Walking with Jesus, a Journey of Transformation

Dova Walker

ROYSTON Publishing

BK Royston Publishing
P. O. Box 4321
Jeffersonville, IN 47131
502-802-5385
http://www.bkroystonpublishing.com
bkroystonpublishing@gmail.com

© Copyright – 2021

All Rights Reserved. No part of this book may be reproduced, stored in a retrieval system, or transmitted by any means without the written permission of the author.

Cover Design: Elite Book Covers

ISBN-13: 978-1-955063-35-7

Printed in the United States of America

TABLE OF CONTENTS

LEARNING TO WAIT UPON GOD   *1*

CHAPTER 1 – THE BEGINNING

1.1	Introduction	*13*
1.2	The Holy Ghost	*15*
1.3	Being Desperate	*18*
1.4	A New Beginning	*23*
1.5	The Journey	*26*
1.6	The List	*29*
1.7	Starting to Date Again	*31*

CHAPTER 2 – DISCOVERY

2.1	Discovery, Introduction	*35*
2.2	Discovery 1994 I, New Realization	*37*
2.3	Discovery 1994 II, Personal Look at Myself	*38*
2.4	Discovery 1994 III, Personal Look 2	*39*
2.5	Discovery 1994 IV, Personal Look 3	*41*

GOD IS AWESOME   *44*

CHAPTER 3 – LEARNING ABOUT MYSELF

3.1	Learning About Myself, Introduction	*45*
3.2	1995, May 8 Taking a Chance by Faith	*47*

3.3	1997, Shedding the Old Man	49
3.4	1999, Feb 25, Learning Things About Myself	51
3.5	2001, Jan 20, Something I Learned About Myself	52
3.6	2001, Jul 2, Today I Begin My Life	54
3.7	2002, Feb 15, Grief over Unfilled Dreams	56
3.8	2005, Jan 15, Cycle of Rebellion	59
3.9	2005, Nov 22, Solution to Cycle of Rebellion	61

THE PREPARATION — (Esther)   **63**

CHAPTER 4 — OVERCOMERS

4.1	Overcomers, Introduction	75
4.2	1999, Jan, Overcoming Jealousy	77
4.3	2000, Don't Miss Your Window of Opportunity	80
4.4	2002, Feb 11, Overcoming Condemnation	82
4.5	2002, Mar 17, Overcoming Faults	83
4.6	2003, Aug 18, The Clean Up	84
4.7	2003, Unrealistic Dreams About Marriage	86
4.8	2005, Mar 30, What Fear Has Caused	88
4.9	2005, Nov 30, Year's End Reflection	89

YOU WOULD RATHER DIE THAN BE WITHOUT ME   **93**

CHAPTER 5 – GOD'S WISDOM KEYS

5.1	God's Wisdom Keys, Introduction	**95**
5.2	This Is Not a Fairy Tale	**97**
5.3	Four Keys to Answered Prayer	**100**
5.4	1998, Gifts That God Wants to Give Us	**101**
5.5	1999, Don't Let the Giants Stop You	**104**
5.6	1999, Questions to Ask Yourself	**105**
5.7	1999, Aug 9, Read the Word, Use the Word, Do the Word	**107**
5.8	2000, Don't tell them your secrets	**108**
5.9	2000, Occupy Till I Come	**110**
5.10	2003, S – I – N	**114**
5.11	2004, March, Fruit of the Spirit	**116**
5.12	2005, Darkness Before the Light	**120**
5.13	2005, Jan 10, Respect vs. Pride	**123**
5.14	2005, Jun 12, Commit Thy Way Unto the Lord	**125**
	Rest in the Lord	**126**
5.15	2007, The Whole Armor of God	**127**

THE POTTER'S HOUSE   **131**

CHAPTER 6 – PROPHECIES FROM THE LORD GOD

6.1	Prophecies – Introduction	**141**
6.2	1995, Prophecy	**142**

6.3	2003, *Pray for yourself*	**144**
6.4	2004 Nov 29, *Delight yourself in the Lord*	**145**
6.5	2005, Sept 12, *My Purpose – The Sorrow of God's Heart*	**148**
6.6	2006, May 8, *A Word from the Lord*	**151**
6.7	200,6 Jun 17, *What the Lord Told Me*	**155**

A PAUSE FOR THE CAUSE — **158**

CHAPTER 7 – THE PROMISES OF GOD

7.1	2005, *My Testimony – Introduction*	**159**
7.2	1998, Sept 2, *Great and Precious Promises*	**162**
7.3	2000, Jan 24, *The Promises of God*	**165**
7.4	2002, Jul 2, *The Four Promises of God*	**168**
7.5	2002, *Isaiah 54*	**170**
7.6	2004, Mar 8, *Four Great and Precious Promises*	**172**

HISTORY (His Story) — **175**

CHAPTER 8 – I AM WHO GOD SAYS I AM

8.1	*I Am Who God Says I Am – Introduction*	**183**
8.2	2002, Dec 26, *Learning to Hit the Target*	**184**
8.3	2004, July 12, *I Am Who God Says I Am*	**186**
8.4	2005, Apr 27, *God's Plan for My Life*	**191**
8.5	2005, May 2, *Realizing Who I Am*	**194**

CHAPTER 9 – THE DREAM

9.1	The Dream – Introduction	**199**
9.2	2003, May 24, The Dream	**200**
9.3	2005, Feb 20, Revelation of a Dream	**204**
9.4	2005, Apr 6, Revelation of a Dream II	**208**
9.5	2007, Mar 20, The Dream II	**211**
HOUSE BEAUTIFUL		***213***
Thank you		***217***

LEARNING TO WAIT UPON GOD

ISAIAH 40:28-31

If you want anything from God, you must learn how to wait upon His timing. God loves to bless His people, and in this Book, you will see some of the different ways that God uses to bless us. You will learn how to hear from God and what to do while you are waiting on Him. You will also learn what to look out for.

There are several things you need to know while learning to wait upon God. First you must have a relationship with Him. To have a relationship with God, you must be born again through Jesus Christ, the Son of the Living God. You must be saved. There is no other way to have a relationship with God. This is not something man set up; it is what God Himself set up. He had a plan for salvation before the world began. He knew that someday man would sin, and He provided for it before it even happened.

Disobedience is a sin against God, a violation of His commandment and it brings about death. It does not just bring physical death but eternal damnation, in Hell. We were created to live for eternity. God did not create us to die, but sin brought death into the world. The only payment for sin is death. It does not matter if it is a little sin or a big one (there is no such thing as little or big when it comes to sin; sin is a violation of God's law whether it is a little white lie or murder). It all carries the same penalty: death.

The only way to prevent going to Hell after death, you must be sinless. The problem is none of us are sinless. "For all have sinned and come short of the glory of God (Romans 3:23 KJV)." Because of this fact, Jesus came down from heaven as a sinless man, because He was fathered by a sinless God and not sinful man and paid the penalty of death by dying on the cross on our behalf.

How this works is this: the children of Israel in the Old Testament times had to take a lamb of the first year that was without blemish and kill it as a sacrifice for their sins. The blood of the unblemished lamb covered their sin for one year. The problem was it only covered their sin it didn't pay for it. Jesus' blood pays the penalty for sin. It does not just cover it; it eliminates it. However, Christ's sacrifice didn't take sin out of the world. Man is still a free agent and is clothed with choice. He can choose to accept the payment that Christ Jesus paid on the cross and be set free from sin and live eternally in heaven after his physical body dies, or he can choose not to accept Him and pay his own penalty for his sins. This means he will spend eternity in Hell after the death of his body because his blood is not unblemished and spotless.

How do you receive salvation? By faith. There are three things that go along with that. First, you must believe that Jesus is the only begotten Son of God and that after Jesus died on the cross, he rose from the dead on the third day and now sits at the right hand of God the Father. Second, you must confess you are a sinner (a transgressor of the laws of God). Third, you must repent, which means change the way you are living and live a life free from bondage to sin.

Once you have done this, you have a relationship with God. After you have that relationship, you have the privilege to talk to God anytime you want. But it also means He has the privilege to talk to you, too. How do you talk to Him? Through prayer.

After accepting God's plan of salvation, you will need to learn how to hear God for yourself. God is speaking to us all the time; the question is, are you listening? God's Word tells us how God spoke through a burning bush, a whirlwind, dreams, angels, and prophets. For example, in 1 Kings 19:9-13, God spoke to Elijah through an angel and a still small voice.

Today God speaks to us in many ways. He speaks to us through His Word, through pastors and teachers, through prophets you might hear on TV or radio. But He also speaks to us directly. When you hear His voice, it will probably sound like your own at first, but once you get used to hearing Him you will recognize the difference. Do not let people tell you that God doesn't speak that way; He just might not speak to them that way, or they weren't paying attention.

He might start with something simple to get you used to hearing His voice. For example, one day I got up and was getting ready to start my day. It was my day off and after spending time in prayer and Bible reading, the urge came to eat breakfast while trying to decide what to do first. I ignored it in the beginning because there was so much to do that day. The urge got stronger and I heard a voice in my heart say, "you need to stop and eat breakfast." I started to ignore it again but recognized that God might have been trying to get my attention, so I stopped and acknowledged that it was God and asked Him what He wanted me to eat. He said that a bowl of cereal would be nice and that it was a beautiful day outside and it would be a good idea to eat it on the porch.

After fixing my breakfast, I went outside on the porch to eat. While eating, I happened to see one of my neighbors outside in front of her house. When she saw me she waved and I waved back. The next thing I knew, she was walking down to my house and we began a conversation. The thing that was odd about it is that up to that point we had never talked before. We were both new in the neighborhood, so when she came down and started talking, it took me aback. As we talked, she started sharing a few things with me and told me that her mother had died and that she blamed God for it because she felt He should have healed her. Well, my experience was similar with my mother, but I didn't blame God. I didn't understand why He didn't heal her but allowed her to die, but when I asked God, He explained to me that she should have died on the operating table during a quintuple-bypass surgery where she had a stroke. But God gave her one year to get her spiritual life in order. During this time, she was confined to a nursing home. Someone told me that God views healing differently than we do in some cases and that sometimes He heals through death.

God gave me to explain to my neighbor that it was possible He knew that if He left her here, she might have suffered from disabilities, pain, or mental impairments but in heaven she is completely healed, no disabilities, no pain, no deformities, or mental impairments and that instead of being here a short time in pain, she is free from sickness for eternity in heaven, because she told me her mother was saved. My advice to her was to make sure she was in right standing with God so she could make it to heaven and see her mother again. My neighbor received that information with joy and said she was glad she came down to talk to me.

The opportunity to comfort her and help her restore her relationship with God might never have come if I had not listened to the voice telling me simply to stop and eat breakfast. God might give you a simple instruction that will lead to an amazing result. If you listen to Him in the small things, it will be much easier to hear Him when the big things come around. Notice the word "when" not "if." Big things are going to happen; it is just a matter of when. Be mindful of what you hear. It just might be God talking.

It is also important to learn the promises of God for you that are in His Word and stand on them. God gave me four promises from His Word; you will read about them later. The beauty of God's Word is that you can depend on it because His Word is true. Also, God cannot lie; it is impossible for Him to lie. When he says something, it has no choice but to come to pass. If God were to say that the sky is green and not blue, the sky would have to turn green. When God speaks, what he says happens. Why? Because when He speaks, His Word (Jesus) goes out to perform it. God knows you personally, so He will give you promises that pertain specifically to you. Ask Him what promises He has for you, and He will show them to you. You must also learn to find out what changes you need to make to be prepared for the blessings God has for you and then make those changes.

Waiting on God does not mean doing nothing while you wait. Don't be lazy. Get busy; do something. Matthew 25:14-30 is a parable that Jesus told about a man who traveled to a far country and distributed talents between three of his servants according to their abilities. When you read the story, you will see how he expected them to do something with what he gave them. Two did as was expected, but one didn't do anything with what he was given and instead hid it away so he could give it back to the man when he returned. When the man returned, he was not pleased with the servant who hid his talent; in fact, he took the talent from him and gave it to one of the other servants.

We all have changes we need to make. If you make the changes God tells you to make when He tells you to make them, you will get the blessings He has for you. If not, you might lose out on what God has for you, like the man that God took away the talent He gave him and gave it to someone else. If you realize that this might be your situation, go to God and ask forgiveness and ask Him to give you another chance. He might just say "yes."

Now we come to an especially important step. BEWARE OF COUNTERFIETS. Make sure it is God talking to you or that what is being presented to you is from God. Don't be afraid to ask for confirmation. Satan knows what we like, and he knows how to counterfeit God's gifts to us. While I was believing in God to send me a husband, many counterfeits came my way. When I finally let God have His way, He told me "Dova, I have plenty of men for my daughters, but they won't wait for me. They go out into the world, find men to marry, and then bring them to me and want me to bless it." He said, "I can't bless that mess."

Now let's stop here. This does not apply to everyone. There are extenuating circumstances. But there are many women who, because they feel there are no good men in the church or they don't like what they see, will go out and get someone that they know is not saved to marry thinking they can change him once they get married. So many women are so desperate that they are willing to take anything just to keep from being alone. I know because I was one of them. You will read about that later. Know this: you cannot change a man, any man. Only God can change someone. So why put yourself through the agony of marrying someone then waiting until that happens? It could take years.

The Bible says, "Be ye not unequally yoked together with unbelievers: for what fellowship hath righteousness with unrighteousness? and what communion hath light with darkness?"

(2 Corinthians 6:14 KJV) Marriage is already hard because you are bringing two different people from different backgrounds together to become one. When you add being unequally yoked into the mix, it makes it much harder. Why? Because Satan uses that person against you because that person is already in his camp even though they don't realize it. But when you are both saved, you have God to go to and ask for help. It is easier because you are both in God's court. That is not to say that all saved people who get married will make it. We know that because the rate of divorce is just as high among saved people as it is among the unsaved. Also, it does not mean that every unequally yoked couple won't make it. What God showed me is this: He knows who the right person is for you. If you trust Him and wait on Him, He will bless you with the right person and it will be worth the wait. Trust me, I know. He did it for me.

As I said, Satan also knows what you like and will try to bring a counterfeit to cause you to miss the one that God has for you. He will look good and seem like the one, but he's not. Something will be wrong. Not that he isn't a good person, he's just not the right person for you. The way to avoid a counterfeit is to bring them before God. Ask Him if this is the one for you and if not to remove that person from your life or show you what you need to see to make the right decision. DO NOT TRUST YOURSELF. Trust God only. You might have to wait, but it will definitely be worth the wait.

The reason I say do not trust yourself is you cannot see into the other person's life. You don't know what is ahead for them or what might be hidden in their past, but God does. He can see things you cannot see. He knows things you are not being told. This does not only apply to a mate but to anything presented to you: a job, position, an opportunity, etc. Whatever it is, God knows the ins and outs of it. He knows what will work and what will not. He knows what is ahead of you. When I wanted to leave my last job, God said, "not now." I found out later that one of the reasons was I needed the insurance they provided. God knew about the surgeries I would have to have and made sure I had the insurance I needed to cover it.

For reasons like that, don't be upset if God says "no." He might just mean not now, or he might know that the thing you are asking for is not good for you. The person you might be looking at for a mate might be abusive. Just because he is fine does not mean he is nice. If God tells you that the person you have presented to him is the right one, then you need to ask Him if this is the right time. Within this book you will read how God blessed me with things, but it took a year to come to pass. The reason is he put it in my spirit then said the time is not yet. I had to learn to wait for the right time. So many times, God tells someone that there is a person He has for them and they go right out and grab them up instead of asking God if the time is right, then when it doesn't work, they can't figure out why.

When God puts something or someone in your heart that He wants to give you, you must pray for that person or thing. You might be ready, but that person or thing might not be ready for you. The position might not be open yet, the person might not be available yet. They might be in a relationship that they might need to be delivered from. NOT SOMEONE ALREADY MARRIED TO SOMEONE ELSE. They might have a friend that they are seeing casually, or they might be involved with their counterfeit. Your prayers for them might possibly be what brings them out of that relationship. How should you pray for them? Ask God what to pray. What He told me to pray was that He would prepare that person for me and that He would prepare me for that person. He also told me to pray that he would remove any obstacles from our lives that would prevent us from accomplishing His purpose in our lives.

The next thing you need to learn about waiting on God is trust Him through the rough times. You are going to have rough times. Times when it seems too hard to wait and you just want to do something. When times get hard talk to God Himself instead of family, friends, or co-workers. Be honest with God; He already knows about it anyway.

Psalm 37:1-8 (paraphrased) teaches us to "Fret not because of evildoers…; Trust in the Lord, and do good…; Delight yourself in the Lord…; Commit your way to the Lord…; Rest in the Lord…; and Cease from anger." When times get tough, this passage of scripture can help take you through. Also stand on the promises He gives you. They can be your rock.

The last thing to learn is if you mess up (sin), REPENT. Do not stay down and do not keep falling. Psalm 37:23-24 (NKJV) says, "the steps of a good man are ordered by the Lord, And He delights in his way. Though he fall, he shall not be utterly cast down; for the Lord upholds him with His hand." If you find yourself weak in an area take it to God. He can help you overcome it. And the beauty of it is He wants to help you overcome it. He wants you to succeed.

Learning to wait on God might not be easy, but it is definitely worth it. God has so much in store just waiting for you. It would be a shame to miss out on what He has for you because you would not ask.

Chapter 1

THE BEGINNING

Introduction 1.1

A journey with God is never without bumps and potholes in the road. I made some mistakes and bad choices along the way but also made some decisions that I am incredibly grateful for. Decisions to make some changes in my life that have affected me to this day and brought me closer to God.

I hope that while you read these pages you will see how important it is to make the right decisions in your life. Wrong choices can cause a lot of damage — sometimes long-range damage that lingers on for years. God can help you fix whatever is wrong. Trust Him and let Him help you make right and profitable decisions that you will not regret later in life.

Reading this book will help you see the difference in your life when you let God have control. It will show how He can take broken pieces and make them whole again. Also, how He can make your dreams come true. You have a part to play. You must make the changes God tells you to make. But trust me: it is worth it. The longer it takes you to make the changes, the harder it can be. If you listen and obey God, you will avoid a lot of pain and heartache.

This book is set up showing different stages of my life as seen throughout my journals. You will see how my thoughts change year by year, how God would show me something and then expand on it as the years went by. Each chapter is chronicled by a subject and the date or year of my thoughts on that subject that started in one year and changed over the course of several years. Also, you will see special inserts between some of the chapters that are packed with amazing insights from God.

Chapter 1
THE HOLY GHOST
1.2

It was a Sunday morning in 1985, my first visit to a Mega Church.

My hairdresser invited me to what turned out to be the most amazing experience of my life, getting filled with the Holy Ghost, an experience I will never forget.

At the end of the service, the Pastor gave an altar call. This altar call was different from other altar calls I remembered. Not only did he ask if there was anyone who wanted to receive Christ as Savior, but he also gave separate altar calls for anyone who wanted to receive the Holy Ghost and another one for anyone wanting to join the church. My hand went up to receive the Holy Ghost because I had already accepted Christ as my Savior.

We were escorted to another location in this huge church and were separated by category: those who wanted to receive salvation, those who wanted to receive the Holy Ghost, and those who wanted to join the church. Each group went to different locations inside the facility. Our group was seated, and they explained that they were going to assign an individual to each of us.

I had no idea who the young lady was who was assigned to me, but I thank God for her. She proceeded to take me through the Bible scriptures and teach me who the Holy Ghost is, His true connection to the Trinity, and what His purpose is in the Body of Christ. Then she explained the scriptures on how to receive the Holy Ghost by faith and the laying on of hands as was done in the book of Acts (Acts 8:14-17) and other scriptures. Then she carefully explained that she was going to pray for me and would lay hands on me in faith to receive the Holy Ghost and that I had to believe by faith to receive Him. She also explained that once she was finished praying that I was to open my mouth and speak.

As she began to pray there was this strange feeling in the pit of my stomach where she had placed her hand. I felt like something was turning around and around in my stomach and it got stronger the longer she prayed. The thought was churning in my mind "if she doesn't finish praying soon, I'm going to throw up." Finally, she said "open your mouth and speak." My mouth opened and these words came out that I had never heard before and did not understand. It was another language and very fluent. Although I did not understand what was being said, there was the sense that it was like a child who had been separated from a parent for many years and just been reunited with him. It was the most wonderful experience of my life.

The lady was trying to explain more to me, but I could not stop speaking. When the Holy Ghost was done, she gave me some literature to take with me to help me better understand what I had just experienced. She told me a special point to remember is that the Holy Ghost is a gentleman and would not embarrass me in public, that he was subject to the person and would not force you to do anything.

Finally, we rejoined the people we came with, and they laughed with joy as I told them what I had experienced. They were so happy for me. This was the beginning of a new relationship with Jesus Christ. God loved me so much that He looked beyond my sinful past and gave me a new way to look at my life, which enabled me to look ahead with joy and gladness.

Chapter 1
BEING DESPERATE
The Dream Killer
1.3

Have you ever met a dream killer? Someone who puts to death all the good things in you or the good things you want to do? That was my ex-husband. We were not married when I received the Holy Ghost, but we married several months later. The whole time we were engaged, God tried to talk me out of it but desperation kept me from listening; it was the worst mistake I ever made.

The experience of receiving the Holy Ghost was so exciting, it was hard to hold it in. I could not wait to get home and share the news with him. He looked at me and said, "It won't last; you'll be back to normal soon." My mouth dropped open and it almost caused me to feel like he had ripped the excitement right out of me, but my being so full of joy made it hard for him to steal the moment away from me.

While growing stronger in the Lord daily, the Dragon "Satan" began to use my then-husband against me. He was an alcoholic, which I did not realize until after we married. My only experience with alcoholics at the time were seeing winos on the corner as I was driving down the street or what I saw on TV shows. There were people in my family who drank, but if they used abusive behavior, I didn't see it, so in my mind they weren't considered alcoholics.

As time went on, things got worse. He became verbally abusive, and the harder I prayed the worse it got. Counseling might have worked except for two things. One: he refused to go with me. He said, "All they will do is tell you to leave me," and two: The counselor who was chosen for me was not the best choice. By the time the session was over, he was basically telling me everything was my fault. Not a good thing to tell someone on their first visit. Needless to say, that was my first and last counseling session. It turned out that at that time the counselor was having his own marital problems and should not have been counseling anyone.

I'm not going to deny that some things were my fault, but until God healed me, in my mind everything was his fault. My efforts to make the marriage work did not turn out as planned. Making sure the house was clean and dinner was ready and making other changes that he complained and yelled about never stopped him from complaining and yelling. To my regret, I even stopped going to church and told God that I wanted to at least be able to say I did everything I could to make the marriage work. My husband had always complained about my never doing the things he wanted to do and kept calling me "holier than thou." All he wanted to do was go to bars, clubs, and casinos for entertainment. To avoid being a hypocrite, I made a choice, although it was the wrong one. My choice was to stop going to church and see if it would help save my marriage.

My ex would watch our Sunday morning church service on TV every week. He told me before we got married that he was saved, but after we were married for a while the realization came that he was not doing any of things the pastor talked about on TV or what the scriptures said to do. He must have thought that watching the program on TV once a week made up for his behavior the rest of the week.

When I stopped going to church and started going to the places he wanted to go, things calmed down some but not for long. He still yelled, complained, and was verbally abusive. He mishandled our finances and got us evicted from our apartment. We found another place to move to and it was actually a better place, but he almost got us evicted from there too except the manager liked me, so he worked with me to keep us from eviction and let me make payments on the past due amount.

Finally, the realization came that even when I did everything he wanted me to do, the way he wanted it done, he still wasn't satisfied and would still complain, yell and be abusive. I knew that if I did not get out of that marriage I would end up in an insane asylum, a prison for killing him or dead myself. Because his abusive behavior was getting worse, the decision to leave him seemed to be the best option. Sometime after leaving him, about a year later, I spoke to his sister who said the family thought he had killed me. Now you know that is awful. I made sure there was no going back and forth and refused to be like some women, who keep going back into abusive relationships. It was certain he was not going to change no matter what I did.

While we were married, his abusive words were like knives killing more and more of me every day. My self-esteem was gone. It was so low that I used to tell people I could have walked under a bed. Considering that I am six feet tall, that is really low. He made me feel like no one wanted me which, after I had left him, caused me to start dating anyone who would ask me out, believing that I did not deserve a good relationship. It caused me to make one stupid mistake after another, even some I am too ashamed to mention.

Finally, one day after a really bad relationship decision, I broke down and told God enough was enough. I was tired of the craziness and wanted my relationship with Him back. To my surprise,

He was right there with open arms to welcome me back like the prodigal son, and He began to talk to me and tell me some amazing things. He never made me feel guilty or ashamed, and said, "All right, you've tried it your way, now try it mine." I have since found out that His way is so much better than mine. The difference is like night and day. What He chose for my life is way better than what I chose for myself.

Chapter 1

A NEW BEGINNING

1.4

One day while I was in prayer, God was talking to me while I was sitting in the middle of my bed with my Bible. He said, "Turn to Isaiah 54." At the time, my Bible reading was not extensive, so I was not even aware that the book of Isaiah had 54 chapters in it. (A bit of trivia, the book of Isaiah has 66 chapters, which is the same number of books that are in the Bible.) While reading chapter 54, a feeling of shock came over me. The realization that everything I was reading was about me. It spelled out my whole life situation. It starts out by saying "Sing, O barren, thou that didst not bear" (KJV). THAT WAS ME, I was childless and at that point I was glad that I did not have any children by my ex-husband.

The scripture goes on to say, "Fear not; for thou shalt not be ashamed: neither be thou confounded; for thou shalt not be put to shame: for thou shalt forget the shame of thy youth..." (Isaiah 54:4 KJV) Forget the shame? You mean that God would remove the shame of my past? That in and of itself was wonderful, but He went on to say He would be my husband and my redeemer. Can you believe that? After the mess I had made of my life, God was willing to be my husband. But I still wondered why, after praying and seeking God for his help with my marriage, it seemed as if he was not there. Nothing I tried worked.

The passage continues to say, "For the Lord hath called thee as a woman forsaken and grieved in spirit, and a wife of youth, when thou wast refused, saith thy God. For a small moment have I forsaken thee; but with great mercies will I gather thee." (Isaiah 54:6-7 KJV) Wow, God, this is what happened. It finally dawned on me that God refused to help me in that marriage because I wasn't supposed to be in it in the first place. I had married for all the wrong reasons. I remember saying to myself, "I'd rather say I'm divorced than to say I've never been married. At least it would seem that someone wanted me." This is probably the same reason many other women have made bad marriage choices.

God revealed to me that while standing there in front of Him and all those people, that I had lied to that man knowing that I did not mean the vows I made. The scripture continues and says, "In a little wrath I hid my face from thee for a moment; but with everlasting kindness will I have mercy on thee, saith the Lord thy Redeemer." (Isaiah 54:8 KJV) God had forgiven me and was not mad at me. As I continued to sit there in the middle of my bed, God began to show me all the bad decisions I had made and why, but he never made me feel ashamed. He showed me what I was really looking for: Love, but I was looking in all the wrong places for all the wrong reasons. I was looking for acceptance and fulfillment. God showed me the right reasons, that He had already accepted me, and that He is the only one that can bring fulfillment, which led me to decide not to date anyone for at least one year. For me that was a long time, but it helped me to re-establish my relationship with God and get reacquainted with myself as well as get a better understanding of relationships and how to make better choices.

Chapter 1
THE JOURNEY
1.5

After I made the decision to stop dating, men came out of the woodwork. Every day for about a week, some tall, dark, and handsome (fine) man would ask me out. Thank God for recognizing the attempts of Satan to make me go back on my decision not to date. Their attempts only made me laugh and say, "no." What was funny was that they were all about five to eight years younger than I was. That makes for a real self-esteem booster. It seems funny how men are attracted to you when you are not even interested in dating.

I got filled with the Holy Ghost in 1985 and rededicated my life back to God ten years later in 1995. The one year of dedication and not dating caused me to learn a lot about myself. Little did I know that this particular year would bring about many changes, like moving back to Springfield, Illinois, after living in California for 14 years. You might be thinking, "if you were in California all that time, why in the world did you come back to Springfield?" Well, there were several reasons. First and foremost, my mother was terribly ill. Second, after she died a year and a half later, it was too hard to leave my dad. Third, in some big cities you meet a lot of people, but do you really know them? Some people who move there re-invent themselves, leaving you unaware of their background. Don't get me wrong, there are a lot of really great people there who have become really great friends. My family there was wonderful, and they are some of the most hilarious people you will ever meet. They kept me in stitches. I miss them.

Still there is nothing like being around people you grew up with. You know their background and their family. You know who to stay away from, and if you're not sure, someone you know does and can help you avoid some bad mistakes. In Los Angeles, unless you make plans to meet somewhere with your friends or family, it is a little rare to just run into people you know. In Springfield, however, you can go to the grocery store and run into people you know but haven't seen in a while. I like that. It makes me glad to be home again.

The fourth and most important reason of all is that it was all ordained by God. He had His reasons for bringing me back to Springfield. I will get to that later. Since being back, God gave me the idea to write down some of our conversations, things He gave me during my prayer time. So, as He gives me things, I write them down. This is the beginning story of my journey with God to prepare me for the Man of God he had in store for me. Waiting for God to prepare you for His plan is not easy but it is well worth it.

Chapter 1

THE LIST

1.6

While I was talking to a friend of mine one day, she told me that when you ask God for something be specific, write it down and present it to Him. At the time, asking God for a husband was foremost on my mind, so I decided to make a list of all the things that were important to me in a husband. My relationship with the Lord had grown and we had been working on how I viewed relationships with men. Jesus helped me get a better understanding of what I was looking for in a husband and told me not to settle for less than His best for me. On that list were things like:

Must be Saved, Sanctified, and filled with the Holy Ghost

Loves God

Tall, dark, and handsome

At least 6' 4"

Good listener

Likes to travel

Must enjoy going places like museums, parks, sightseeing, etc.

Has a white-collar job with a blue-collar heart and carries a briefcase

Built like a football player

Likes to work out

Owns his own house

Makes at least $50,000 per year

Must be able to make me laugh

Has a soft side but still masculine

Does not drink, smoke, or do drugs

Doesn't watch sports all day

Knows how to treat women

Good dresser

Smart

Good with money

Not a womanizer

Has a gentle nature

Likes going to church and church functions

Not abusive or argumentative

Confident and secure in himself but not prideful

There was much more on my list than what is written here, but this is an example of what was presented before God to let Him know what I wanted in a husband. I tried to be as specific as possible while believing by faith to receive everything I asked for.

Chapter 1
STARTING TO DATE AGAIN
1.7

In the previous pages, I wrote about taking a year off from dating. God taught me a lot about myself during that year. He taught me my likes and dislikes about myself and about men. Also, to stop settling for less than His best for me and that I had been dating men that had some of the characteristics on my list but many that were not on the list; they might be smokers, or they might drink a little or do other things that were not characteristics of a godly man.

The Lord let me know that I did not have to settle for the things I do not like just to get the things I do like. He said it was possible to have everything in one person. Jesus told me that most people say that a relationship must be a 50/50 love. God said not so. He said each person must be willing to give 100%. Never put just 50% into the relationship or it will never work.

The Lord showed me that there were certain things to look for in a godly man. Then He told me to get out my list and I thought, "Great, Jesus is going to give me the man of my dreams." I got out my list and the Lord said, "Let's go over it." As we went over all the items on my list God said, "I want you to get a picture in your mind of exactly what this man looks like." So. the vision in my mind was a tall, dark, and handsome man in an expensive dark suit with a white shirt and a nice tie. He looked like a famous actor and my image of him was that of a lawyer or an executive for a big company who would go to the gym every day to work out. Someone who might have important political connections or something. Then God asked me a question. He said, "Now considering all that you imagine him to be, do you measure up to the kind of woman this type of man would be looking for?" WHAT!!! My mouth fell open.

I could see in my mind the type of woman that a man like that would be interested in (about 5' 8", exceptionally beautiful, long hair, very shapely, very fit, someone who also likes to work out and is highly active, a businesswoman making lots of money). That is not me. I stand 6' tall, very thin, and I do not work out. Also, my income would not be considered making lots of money, and you would probably consider me average looking. So, the answer to God's question was no, I was lacking in what I thought a man like that would be looking for. Then the Lord said, "okay, then we need to tweak your list." So that meant narrowing it down. So I narrowed it down to Saved, Sanctified, and filled with Holy Ghost, and he also must be tall, dark and handsome *__to me__*. I decided then that the rest was not really that important.

After that, the Lord began to show me what was important. Finding a man who was Saved, Sanctified, and filled with the Holy Ghost was most important of all. Then he needed to be a true man of God who loves the Lord with all his heart. Someone with integrity and morals, someone who lives a life of holiness. Someone who is active in the church. These are the things that are important. The Lord said that if I would trust Him, He would bless me with a man of God who would love me and cherish me, and He told me exactly how he would treat me.

Now that the one year has ended and my decision is made to begin dating again, I start with a new view of men, a new view of myself and a new appreciation for who I am becoming, also a stronger realization that I deserve better for myself than what I had previously chosen. Now there is no more settling for less than God's best for me. My faith assures me that He will bless me.

UPDATE

In 2006 the Lord blessed me with the husband I always wanted. Not only is he Saved, Sanctified, and filled with the Holy Ghost, but to me he is very handsome and everything on my list that I wanted. There were a few things that were different, such as one of the items on my list was being a white-collar man with a blue-collar heart, which means being sophisticated but down to earth. So, for his white-collar job he wears a minister's collar, and the briefcase he carries is a saxophone case. And even though he is a very sharp dresser, his regular job is in a factory which gives him that blue-collar heart. God has a sense of humor.

Chapter 2
Introduction 2.1
DISCOVERY

Self-discovery is a process, and these next pages are my opportunity to share with you the amazing journey of self-discovery that the Lord brought me through. By my writing things in a journal, He helped me face things about myself that I did not like, things I learned to appreciate, and things I did not even know. It was a discovery of things about me that had been hidden for years. There are things I faced for the very first time and things that were hidden that were brought to the surface.

The Lord Jesus also helped me to see myself in the past. He helped me to recognize what needed changing in my life, the areas of my life where deliverance was needed and which areas He was developing. The time frame of this next chapter takes place one year before I rededicated my life back to God and starting to date again and are entries in my journal.

When I look back at all the Lord brought me through, I see so much growth. I hope these pages will help you take a closer look at yourself and see what God might want to change in you. Before you can be in a healthy relationship with others you have to be healthy yourself. Get to know yourself. Discover who you are in God and who he is in you. Have fun on the journey. It might not be easy, but as I've said before, it is definitely worth it. Trust the Lord to go through the journey with you. He knows more about you that you know about yourself.

Chapter 2
DISCOVERY 1994 I
A New Realization
2.2

It's about 1:30 in the morning and I can't sleep for thinking about my life and realizing it needs some direction, some goals to work for and meaning. Right now, there is no one special in my life to give me purpose or a reason for doing things. I realize that I do not need anybody to make me happy or to fulfill my life, but I need something. Goals must be set, or nothing will get done. I also need discipline. I NEED JESUS.

All this time I have been escaping from something not knowing what. I realize now it is commitment, commitment to God and to myself. Because of past failures, there is the fear that I might fail again, so I must get rid of the fear of getting my relationship with Jesus back, so I can enjoy the fellowship, trust, sense of peace, direction, understanding, and commitment.

Sometimes it gets hard to see the forest for the trees. I get so caught up in the little things it makes it difficult to see the big picture. I know it will all come together. I just hope it happens soon.

Chapter 2
DISCOVERY 1994 II
A Personal Look at Myself
2.3

I have to stop being everybody's door mat and stop daydreaming about what my life should be like. Now is the time to start living the life God wants me to live. Sometimes I get afraid of being alone and sometimes it can be a welcome change. I need to get used to being my own person and learn to enjoy doing things without worrying about who to do them with. There is so much in life to enjoy and now is the time to start enjoying it.

I need to stop being afraid. There is nothing to be afraid of. My mother taught me that whatever I want to be in life I can be, so I think I should make that my focus. Too much time has been spent worrying about the fact that I do not have children, that I live alone, and am working at a job that is not to my liking right now. There is a reason for me to be here, I just need to find it. There is something I should be doing and with God's help, I'll figure it out in His time.

Chapter 2
DISCOVERY 1994 III
A Personal Look 2
2.4

Where is my life going? Nowhere. It seems that I am not doing anything of importance; I am not helping anyone or making any contributions. Everyone needs to feel needed, to be important to someone. I am not feeling either. My life feels wasted. My job is not important to anyone. It doesn't seem to mean anything.

There seems to be a large gap between my knowledge and the things that are important. It seems hard for me to sit and hold an intelligent conversation with people. If they are talking about computers, finances, mortgages, children, investments, or politics, my ability to relate to what they are referring to is limited. There is too much time spent daydreaming about a life I might never have because I won't get up and do anything with the life I've got.

Sometimes it seems like I'm trapped, like I should be happy with what I have, but at the same time it's getting me nowhere. Sitting and thinking about what to do with my life is hard because I don't have any idea of how or where to start. I suppose I do but I'm scared to try. Maybe the first thing should be to get a daytime job instead of my current evening job, so I could go to school at night to learn computers or maybe interior design. Well, that seems like a great place to start.

Chapter 2
DISCOVERY 1994 IV
A Personal Look 3
2.5

It's 12:41 a.m. and I learned something very special this morning. I must find the me who was lost years ago behind men. I used to dream about my future; it was so exciting. I was creative, always making things, building things, and designing things. Where did all that go? My artistic talent seems to have gotten lost; my desire for it has changed into a desire to chase after the allure of marriage and finding a husband, thinking a husband held the key to my happiness. Now I know that the only one who holds that key is me.

God gave me a talent, an inner beauty and strength. I must use it to make my own happiness. It will be better to focus on my parents' love and what they taught me, and to learn of God's love and what it teaches me, how it can fill me, and how it can help me grow. Men are of no importance right now. They are only hindrances in my life until I find myself again.

Another thing is laziness; it seems that it tried to take control of me, keeping me from achieving my dreams. But now I know that it is a spirit that must be bound in order for me to retake control of my life and understand how to use the authority given to me through Christ in order to avoid it trying to take control again.

Because of letting go of my dreams, there was no purpose or direction to my life, no desires, no goals to give me reason to get up and do something. I would say to myself why do it now, it will wait until tomorrow; it doesn't affect anybody but me; it's not that important. Now I realize that I am that important, that I matter, that there is a reason for me to be here, that God loves me no matter what. I'm His child and His desire is to make me the best person I can be.

REFLECTION

GOD IS AWESOME

God is so awesome, amazing, and wonderful. I love Him so much. He listens to me and then takes the time to answer my prayers and my questions. He loves me so much and I can really begin to see it.

No man can love me the way the Lord does, and no man can do for me what God can. He is so amazing, and I am thankful He's in my life. I have always looked for love and now I have found it in Jesus. Just watching the things He's done in my life is most amazing, how He delivered me from a bad situation by helping me face it, stay there, and not run. Then He gave me complete deliverance in it. He listens to me and then within hours or a few days answers my prayer and how He lifts me up when I'm down, encourages me to keep trying, supplies my needs, and allows me to be used for His glory.

He has helped me develop relationships with people and has restored old ones. I am so glad that God loves me and wants to use me for His glory. Lord, help me stay humble before you and others so people will only see Christ in me.

Chapter 3

Introduction 3.1

LEARNING ABOUT MYSELF

The power of this next chapter is in the revelations I received from God. These revelations taught me a lot about myself, that not everything is good, but I have learned from each of them. Learning about yourself is not an easy thing to do. There are things that you learn that you do not like, and you must face those things in order to overcome them.

What you learn about yourself is key to moving forward in God. How you face your fears, your disappointments, and your hang-ups can cause a change in your life that can have ripple effects. It can change the way you see yourself and the way others see you.

One thing I learned about God is that He will not condemn you for your past, but He is willing to help you change your future. If you are feeling condemned, it is not by God. Satan is the accuser of the brethren and he is the one who causes you to feel condemned. The Holy Ghost will bring conviction when you sin but that is to bring you to repentance; conviction is different from condemnation. Once you repent, the conviction goes away. Satan, however, wants you to stay in the state of condemnation.

The love of God is so powerful that it overcomes condemnation and brings you peace, and when you are at peace with God, you _can_ face anything. As the scripture says, "I _can_ do all things through Christ which strengthens me." (Philippians 4:13 NKJV) Use this powerful weapon of warfare against Satan when he tries to use your shortcomings against you to bring you into condemnation. Never forget you _can_ overcome your fears, you _can_ overcome disappointments, and you _can_ overcome your hang-ups for "…we are more than conquerors through Him that loved us." (Romans 8:37 KJV)

Chapter 3
TAKING A CHANCE BY FAITH
May 8, 1995
3.2

Today God taught me something incredibly special: He loves me and is looking out for me. My decision to take a chance by faith and quit my job was weighing heavy on my mind and left me wondering if it was the right thing to do or not and if I had truly heard from God or not. Well, today I know for sure it was God.

During prayer this morning, God put the story of the rich young ruler in my heart to look up. While doing so, it was amazing how He took me right to the scripture, Luke 18:18-30. It was a confirmation of many things but the main one is this: what is impossible with man is possible with God. I realize now that the reason quitting my job worried me so much was because although God told me to quit the job, there was not a Word from God to go with it, to back it up. This scripture gave me that Word. Through it He has shown me that He's with me, that He cares about what I do and that He is here to help me through it.

At the end of this story in Luke, Jesus talks about how no

one leaves house or parent or family for the kingdom of God's sake who will not receive manifold more in this present time and in the world to come life everlasting. So, this let me know that obeying God and leaving my job is like leaving house or parent or family in the eyesight of God. Why, because I was too dependent on that job, now it was time to take a chance by faith and depend on God.

Throughout this, I have learned how important the Word of God is, because it literally gives me strength to accomplish my goals. It gives confirmation, instruction, and direction. It also heals and restores. It is truly the LIVING Word of God.

Chapter 3
SHEDDING THE OLD MAN
1997
3.3

God is taking me through changes right now. Although I am not sure what all they involve, I do know I'll be victorious in it and that God will take me to a higher level in Him and help me grow spiritually to become more like Jesus. This process involves shedding the old man and putting on the new man.

God is perfecting me, molding me, and shaping me – changing me into who He wants me to be. God is calling me to obedience to Him, to be a doer of the Word and not a hearer only. However, the fear of failing Him again has caused me to operate in fear.

I have been afraid that Satan will use things against me to cause me to leave the church as he used my ex-husband against me several years ago, but God did not give me a spirit of fear but of power and of love and of sound mind. (2 Timothy 1:7 paraphrased) Since this fear is part of the old man, using the power of God to overcome it will allow me to exercise the authority given to me as the new man through Christ Jesus.

Chapter 3

LEARNING THINGS ABOUT MYSELF

February 25, 1999

3.4

Learning about too many negative attributes in my life has caused me to really take a look at myself. When I am weak and recognizing carelessness in my life, it is a great opportunity for God to show Himself strong in me. God says I do not have to stay this way. I can change what I am.

The best part is that I know He will help me because His Word says, "The Lord will perfect that which concerneth me: thy mercy, O Lord, endureth forever: forsake not the works of thine own hands." (Psalm 138:8 KJV) So He will help me become the best person I can be for Him. It will take discipline and a lot of prayer, but I can change. I am looking forward to becoming a better person.

Chapter 3
SOMETHING ELSE I LEARNED ABOUT MYSELF
January 20, 2001
3.5

God is teaching me so much about myself. He is showing me that I have never been happy with myself and always wanted to change who I am. As a teenager, I often daydreamed about myself in a different life, the same family but living a different life.

There was always the temptation, as I grew older, to want to be like someone else instead of being content with myself. There was always a great admiration for other people who seemed to be outgoing and popular. They always seemed so confident in who they are, and people were always attracted to them. This has been happening for so long that I do not really know myself anymore because of trying to pattern my life after others, even my mother.

Now that I have been asked to be in certain positions like head of an auxiliary or leader of a group, I'm finding it very hard because there is no one to pattern myself after, therefore I'm lost and unsure what to do and don't know how to proceed or what steps to take next. There is the fear of failure and the fear of success. Where do I go from here?

Thanks be to my God and Father and the Lord Jesus Christ. He alone has helped me come to this revelation of myself. He knows which way I should go and which way I will go, because He designed me, made me, and fashioned me to be who I am. God knows the difference between who He created me to be and who I am now. I love the Lord and thank Him for making me the person He designed me to be. I am like no one else and no one else is like me.

Chapter 3
TODAY I BEGIN MY LIFE
July 2, 2001
3.6

Once again, the Lord showed me something about my life, He showed me why my success as a leader has failed. For too many years, I have been a follower, working on jobs as an assistant manager but never a manager, always assisting and following a set plan instead creating my own plan. My education in fashion design taught me how to be a leader, but my work history only allowed me to assist leaders. Instead of putting my focus to good use and learning how to become a successful store manager or business owner, I put all my concentration and focus on finding the right man to marry and beginning my fairy tale life. I thought "As soon as I find my husband, my fantasy life will begin." Well, I got married but not to the man of my dreams, so here I am 41 years old, divorced from an abusive man, and still waiting for my fairy tale life to begin. NOT ANYMORE.

My life begins today. I know that I'm a child of the Most High God, a child of the King, a jewel in His crown, His precious daughter, and I belong to Him. God wants to give me all the things I have dreamed about so I can tell other women that they don't have to wait on a man to fulfill their dreams. That they can trust in God to fulfill any dreams they might have.

Chapter 3
GRIEF OVER UNFULFILLED DREAMS
February 15, 2002
3.7

Several months ago, I went through a grieving period over the loss of unfulfilled dreams in my life. As a teenager with my whole life ahead of me and a talent for art, I dreamed of being a fashion designer, decorator or architect. It was fun making model houses out of different types of boxes like dress boxes or shoe boxes or small appliance boxes, etc. That led to an interest in architecture, but my math skills were lacking, so that caused me to settle for a career in fashion design. It seemed like a very exciting opportunity. So that was my career choice and what I went to college for. I also hoped that I would get married to the man of my dreams. He would be tall, dark, handsome, and rich. We would buy a house and have children. In fact, most of my free time as a teenager was spent daydreaming about it.

After graduating from college, a job opportunity in the retail fashion industry opened that made me think, "I'm on my way". It's normal to work your way up to what you want to be, in my case a fashion designer, however I had no idea that working retail would never get me there.

When an opportunity came to move to the west coast it made me think once again that I was on my way to my dream life. My first move was to Seattle, Washington then about a year later it was on to sunny southern California, a place I had always dreamed of moving to. Having family in both places really helped, but the big city is so different. I was able to travel to some great places and a friend of mine who is a designer let me do some modeling for her. That was very exciting, but it didn't lead me to becoming the fashion designer of my dreams.

The dream of getting married was also a failure. The man I married was definitely not the man of my dreams. His abusive behavior led to getting a divorce, and my eventual move back to my hometown. The dream of having children also never came to pass. In fact, none of the plans for my dream life had come to pass. It was very painful to realize that my dreams had not been fulfilled.

One day, while in prayer, the Lord asked me about the plan for my dream life and where did I think those dreams came from. WOW! I never thought about where they came from, but with my love for art, fashion and design it just seemed that it was the right fit for me. God said "I gave you those dreams. That is what I wanted for your life, but you went out to try and accomplish them without me. You can't do that. That is why you failed." He said, "now it's time to give up your dreams and let them go." WHAT! that hit hard. I cried for two weeks. How do you give up on your dreams if that's all you have to hold on to? Without a dream, what are my goals? What is there to look forward to? Where do I go from here? Finally, God said "I didn't say give up **on** your dreams, I said give up your dreams and let them go." Then it hit me: He meant let go of the tight hold I had on them and give them **up** to Him. He said, "If you give your dreams to me, I will help you to accomplish all of them."

I went out to try and accomplish my dreams on my own and only found Satan's counterfeits, which led to disappointment, deception, loss of self-esteem, frustration, and many other issues. However, God has taken the broken pieces of my life and put them back together and made something beautiful of my life.

****Update****

In November 2002, the Lord blessed me to buy a beautiful house, and, as I have mentioned before, in June 2006, He blessed me with a wonderful husband who is everything I asked God for. In 2013 he blessed me with a job doing In-home decorating.

Chapter 3
CYCLE OF REBELLION
January 15, 2005
3.8

There is a pattern of behavior that the Lord revealed to me, a cycle of rebellious behavior. I'm supposed to do something constructive but instead choose to do something non-constructive, like going to the burger house instead of coming home and eating something I already have, which would have saved me money, but instead I used my credit card to buy it.

When I came home instead of cleaning the house, taking down Christmas Tree or reading something encouraging I sat down and watched TV. My excuse was being sleepy, which was true because sleep sometimes escapes me at night, however it was just an excuse not to do anything.

Later the feelings of guilt about my behavior start kicking in and here is where the cycle begins. Because of feeling guilty, I begin to try figuring out a defense and a way to repent and ask God for forgiveness. Then comes examining myself to figure out why this happens, what is wrong with me, etc. Then comes trying to figure out the cause of all the problem like not sleeping at night. Why is that? Maybe because God is trying to get my attention. Then sometimes there is the "if only" stage; for example, I think "if only I could be more like this person or that person"; but that makes me realize how much I compare myself to other people when I should only compare myself to Christ.

After going through this brief self-examination, the realization comes that I will just keep falling into the same pattern all over again and the same thing tomorrow or a few days from now. Then it came to my attention, I should say it was God who brought it to my attention, that I have been meditating on the problem instead of meditating on God's Word concerning the problem. The only way I am going to overcome problems and stop focusing on myself is to meditate on God's Word and concentrate on others, not on what they are doing but on how to be of service to them. One way to do this is to write things down that I fall habit to and find a scripture that overcomes it and concentrate on that. Also find scriptures that focus on being of service to others and meditate on them.

Chapter 3
SOLUTION TO CYCLE OF REBELLION
November 22, 2005
3.9

Back in January 2005, God brought a pattern of behavior to my attention, a cycle of rebellious behavior. In June, He gave me the solution to the problem, but it was not until November that I recognized that the two go together. Right now, I am struggling with the pattern of behavior that I want to break and tonight the Lord showed me the solution.

In June, God taught me how to break that cycle by standing on His Word using Psalm 37. To do this I have to **Commit my way unto the Lord** (vs 5), turn over to Him my behavior, give it into His care. I must **Delight myself in the Lord** (vs 4), which means to **Trust in the Lord** (vs 3) to keep His Word. The fear of messing things up has kept me from being **Strong in the Lord and in His ability to keep me intact.** (Ephesians 6:10 paraphrased) But tonight, I surrender it to Him and entrust myself to His care and ability to keep me.

REFLECTION

THE PREPARATION – Esther

I remember several years ago after reading the story of Esther, how it impressed me so that they spent twelve months preparing the women before allowing them to go in to meet the king. They spent six months using oil of myrrh and six months using sweet odors and other things for the purifying of the women (Esther 2:12). I wondered why it took so long, but when I think about it, they had rounded up women from various cultures and backgrounds. They probably had to be taught how to present themselves to the king, how to talk, how to walk and dress properly and how to conduct themselves overall. If the king was going to delight himself in her she would have to be at her best. She only gets one night with the king, only one chance. If he does not delight in her, she will never be called to see him again.

As I thought about this, it made me think about how God allows the Holy Ghost to prepare us for out meeting with him one day when we either pass into eternity through death or through the rapture. But we are all going to be presented before the King of Kings and Lord of Lords one day. We only get one shot at this. If we are prepared (saved, sanctified, and filled with the Holy Ghost), then the King will delight in us and we will live with Him throughout eternity, but if not (we are not saved), he will not delight in us and we will never see his face. We will spend all eternity separated from Him in Hell.

This part of the story is an amazing representation of the life of the believer. Just as the maidens had to heed the things that Hegai, the keeper of the women, said so they could be prepared to go before the king, so do we have to heed the things that the Holy Ghost says to be prepared to go before our heavenly King.

Let's go back and look at the story. To paraphrase, the story begins with the king of Persia whose name was Ahasuerus who lived in a palace called Shushan. He held a feast in the third year of his reign. The feast was for many princes, nobles, dignitaries, and even his servants. The feast lasted seven days after the king had finished showing off his kingdom for 180 days.

During that time, the queen, whose name was Vashti, also held a feast for the women. The king commanded his servants to bring the queen before him. He wanted to show off her beauty, but the queen refused to come at his command. This was an embarrassment to the king because it happened in front of all his guest. It was stated that not only was the wrong done to the king but to all the princes and all the people of the province in that when the other wives heard what Queen Vashti had done, they might try to dishonor their husbands in the same manner. Because of this, the king commanded that Queen Vashti never be brought before him again and he rejected her as queen.

As time went on the king began to miss Vashti. His advisers suggested that young virgins be rounded up from throughout the province and brought to the palace, from which he could choose a new queen. So, the kings officers went out throughout the province and rounded up all the virgins in the kingdom and brought them to the palace. Among them was a young Jewish girl named Hadassah (Esther), who was being raised by her cousin Mordecai after her parents, Mortdecai's uncle and aunt, had died. Mordecai advised Esther not to tell anyone of her heritage.

After being in the palace, she obtained favor in the sight of the eunuch who oversaw the women, and he gave her the best place in the house of women and provided her with everything she needed. Now as I said before, every woman had a turn to go into the king but before she did, she spent twelve months in preparation, six months with oil of myrrh and six months with sweet spices. After this, she was allowed to take whatever she wanted in with her to see the king. After her night with the king, she was sent to the second house of women where the concubines were kept, and she never came before the king again unless he called for her by name. Esther found favor with the king and was made queen of Persia instead of Vashti.

Now the story goes on from there but let's look again at the time of preparation. There have been several times when God spent time preparing me for the blessing He had for me and it usually took a year. Before I bought my car, the Lord God spoke to me about it. He told me where to go to get the financing and how much to pay for it. I went to find the car I wanted, but the price was higher than I wanted to pay. The Lord told me if I waited one year, the price would come down to the price I wanted to pay. Sure enough, after a year had passed, I went out again and found the very car I wanted for the price I wanted to pay the year before.

When I was ready to buy a house, the Lord God put it in my heart to go looking for a house, but the time was not yet. But one year later, the Lord said it was time and He helped me find a Realtor and where to go to get the financing and helped me find someone who could answer questions for me and help me understand what questions I needed to ask about purchasing a home. The Lord did it again when He brought me to my husband. He put it in my heart who he wanted for me but told me the time was not yet. One year later, God told me it was time and set up the circumstances for us to meet.

With each situation, God waited one year. During that time, He prepared me for the blessing He had in store for me. He prepared me spiritually, mentally, and physically. Spiritually by helping me increase my faith. He told me what He wanted to bless me with and helped me stand by faith to receive it. He gave me scriptures to stand on like the four promises in chapter seven and other scriptures like Psalm 37, which teaches you what to do while you are standing on the Word by faith. Ephesians chapter 6 teaches us about how to be strong in the Lord while we wait and many other scriptures.

God prepares us mentally by teaching us to change the way we think, how we see things, the way we look at life and how people are damaged by the lies Satan has told us. We see ourselves as inferior or not good enough because Satan has perpetuated the lies that we are too fat, too skinny, not tall enough, too tall, we don't have enough hair, or we are too stupid or too dark. If we are smart, then we are labeled negatively and so on.

We are made in the image of God and however we are made is perfect to him. I know there are people with disabilities but even they are perfect to him. It is not about how we look on the outside but who we are on the inside. We need to stop seeing ourselves as the world does and see ourselves as God does.

Have you ever met someone who was quite beautiful on the outside, but you could not stand being around them because they are so mean and hateful on the inside? I have met many people who on the outside were not what the world would consider incredibly attractive but have the best personality and sweetest demeanor. You like being around them because they make you feel good about yourself. They let you be you, but they do not tear you down or make you feel less than others. It is not that you look better than them or have more than they do, it is just that they are comfortable and confident in who they are, and they make you feel comfortable, too.

When we stop seeing ourselves through other people's eyes, we can begin to see ourselves for who we really are. God told me once that we are always critical of ourselves, we don't like this about ourselves or we don't like that, it is as if we are telling God, he made a mistake and made us wrong. That He should have made us like this person or that person. God said that thought is a slap in His face. He has made us the way He wants us to be made and He has a purpose for it. We just need to be thankful and ask God what He wants us to do with how He made us.

This brings me to the physical. God prepares us physically to do his will. He made us a certain way so that we are physically able to carry out His plan for us. He prepares our bodies for such things as having children, you never know if you might be the one raising the next President of the United States, or the next brilliant scientist or doctor, or even a great poet or schoolteacher. You never know who God has entrusted you with. Do you think Mary's mother knew she was raising the child who would be the mother of the Savior of the world? What about Martin Luther King Jr's mother, did she know who she was raising?

Some people are of a short or a small stature. There are many occupations and places where they are more suited than someone tall. For example, in the horse racing industry, jockeys are usually of a short or small stature; they are more suited for this job than a tall person. How can God reach someone in this industry? By placing one of his children there, i.e., a small person as a jockey. Someone whom other jockeys can relate to. Basketball players are usually very tall, and God can use a tall person in that industry to reach other players. It is usually a lot easier to reach someone for Christ when you have things you can both relate to. What about women who no longer have the Coke bottle figure they had in their youth? Other women who have had this problem who are children of the Most High God can relate to them and show them what God can do in their lives. He might not change their shape, but He can help them see themselves differently, help them to appreciate themselves the way they are.

This book is filled with the things the Lord God taught me about how to trust in Him for everything, like how to trust Him to change my habits, my conversation, my ways and my thoughts. Also, how to recognize negative patterns in my life such as pride, gossip, anger, the need to be in control, and a few other things. After recognizing these things, He helped me overcome them. Now they no longer control me. I still have to deal with them from time to time, but now I know what they are and how to pay attention when they pop up so I can cast them down and use the Word of God against them.

For example, when I recognize the spirit of pride popping up, I first turn to God and repent and ask for forgiveness. Then I bind that spirit of pride by using the scripture that teaches us that we have the power to tread on serpents and scorpions and over all the power of the enemy. (Luke 10:19 paraphrased) Also whatsoever we bind on earth will be bound in heaven and whatsoever we loose on earth shall be loosed in heaven. (Matthew 16:19 paraphrased) Then I ask God to release (loose) the fruit of the Spirit in my life (meekness).

The scripture also tells us to "Submit yourselves therefore to God. Resist the devil, and he will flee from you." (James 4:7 KJV) This means if you stay in the presence of God the enemy will run away because he doesn't want to stay under God's presence and scrutiny. He likes to keep you in the dark away from God. This is why it is so important to turn to God right away when you have sinned or fallen to temptation. The longer you stay under that condition, the more time Satan has to plant wrong thoughts in your mind, to make you feel condemned instead of convicted by the Holy Ghost. There is a difference. Satan also uses that time to tempt you to sin again. He will try to convince you that you are no longer saved, that God is angry with you and won't take you back after what you have done, that everyone is talking about you, etc. All these are lies that Satan will try to use to draw you away from God. He cannot snatch you out of God's hand, but he will try to convince you to leave God.

Satan has no power over you, but he will try to influence you against God or deceive you into making wrong decisions that cause you to sin against God. You need to stay mindful of his devices, stay prayerful and repent quickly. God knows what you did anyway and is waiting on you to come to Him so He can cleanse you from that sin, pick you up from the fall and set you back on your feet so you can continue to walk with Him. He is not angry when you fall, but

He does not want you to stay there. He wants you to get up and keep going.

Have you ever watched a baby who is learning to walk? They fall a lot, but they get up and keep trying until they are no longer falling all the time but are walking successfully. The next thing you know, they're running everywhere. We are like that; in the beginning we fall a lot and sometimes we stay there and have a pity party but we, by the grace of God, get up and keep going, and the more we succeed, the more our faith grows. The more our faith grows, the less we fall, and the less we fall, the more we run on for God.

What does this have to do with preparation? A lot. When God is preparing you for something, He has to first help you see the things that are hindering you and help you get rid of them. Like the women in the palace, we have to be prepared. This is the six months with oil of myrrh, not literal six months but figurative. God spends time healing us from the effects of sin. Then he spends time adding to us the attributes that are more like Him; this is the six months of sweet spices. God begins to teach us how to walk in the fruit of the Spirit, use the Word of God, and use our authority over Satan.

The Lord God is preparing us to ultimately spend eternity with Him, but in the meantime, He blesses us with things along the way. It might be a new car, a new house, or other things like a new job, raise, or promotion. But these are small things. He also blesses us with even greater things like the salvation of family, friends, and loved ones. He blesses us with new people in our lives like a wonderful husband or children. The best is a new life in Christ.

It is one thing to have lots of stuff but quite another to have a new life. There are many people with a lot of things who are not happy. They are miserable. They have to watch their backs all the time, they can't trust people. Many can't even trust family. They are angry all the time and many are mean and controlling. They think nothing of using people and stepping on people to get what they want. Some will even kill those who get in their way. Many use deceptive practices in business and will prefer to lie than to tell the truth.

When we allow God to make the changes in us that He wants to make and to prepare us for the things He has in store for us, we too like Jesus will be patient, kind, and loving to others; we will use good manners, have joy and peace with God, be gentle and humble and use self-control, and most of all we will increase our faith in God. Now that is how the fruit of the Spirit is evident in our lives. We cannot do this on our own. We can only do this through salvation through Christ Jesus and being filled with the Holy Ghost. The Holy

Ghost is like Hegai, the keeper of the women in the palace of King Ahasuerus. He prepares the women for their one night with the king. Only unlike King Ahasuerus, who could only find delight in one woman to be made queen, the Lord God our Father finds delight in all who accept His Son Christ Jesus as their savior and allows us to live with Him in heaven for eternity. I pray that you will see how God is preparing you for His blessing now and for all eternity.

Chapter 4
Introduction 4.1
OVERCOMERS

I want to help you learn about overcoming problems, faults, attributes, and ways that are not pleasing to God. Sometimes you must take a good look at yourself to understand what you need to change. You will find that some of them are not pleasing. In fact, they can be downright ugly and hard to face but if you trust God and allow Him to help you take a really good look at yourself no matter how ugly it can be, you will find that He will help you make the changes in yourself that you want and need to make.

God is calling us to be the best we can be. You do, however, need to make sure you are becoming the best you possible. Don't try to be someone else. God created each of us to be unique. So, do not try to imitate anyone else. No one can be who you are, and you cannot be anyone else.

You are fearfully and wonderfully made (Psalm 139:14) and God loves you just the way you are, so learn to love yourself. But there are certain things God put in you for him to use for this day and time. No one else is supposed to do what God put in you to do.

It could be singing, preaching, teaching, administration, comforting, helping others, or drawing others to Christ. There are people that God puts in our lives to reach for Christ that others cannot reach. It might be family members or people on your job, your manicurist, hairdresser, next-door neighbor, or mailman.

Being effective for Christ means overcoming hindrances, which makes you an effective tool that He can use to reach others. He will use your experience to relate to others who are experiencing the same problem. That opens an opportunity to tell them how God helped you overcome it and that if He helped you, He could help them too.

So, as you read these next entries you will see where God helped me to recognize the problems I needed to overcome. I hope that by reading this, you will see yourself and the things God is trying to show you. Your experience might be different but the process to overcome, recognize, acknowledge, and change
should be the same; be blessed.

Chapter 4
OVERCOMING JEALOUSY
January 1999
4.2

Jealousy seems to keep plaguing me. It seems as soon as I thought it was under control, it pops up again. It began with a project that was assigned to me that I received no recognition for. Someone was assigned to help me with the project who started trying to take control of it and then proceeded to push me out of it. Sure enough, that person received all the recognition for it as if my participation had nothing to do with it and didn't even mention my part in the project.

Then it was an idea that God had given me that someone took over after I had shared it with them and then they prevented me from even being able to participate in it. Next it was a relationship that didn't go as expected then someone else started received the attention that was once mine. Before anything else comes upon me, my hope is to learn from God, my Father, how to overcome this and be healed.

First: Recognize that it is jealousy and envy.

Second: To recognize what my feelings are about it.

- My desire was to show my ability in regard to the project that was assigned to me and wasn't really aware that the other person wanted the same thing.
- I was upset that the person did not even acknowledge that the idea was mine and proceeded as if it was theirs and then told me my presence was no longer needed.
- My feelings were really strong for the person from the relationship and my desire was to continue in the relationship but ended it because God instructed me to do so but it was very hard to get over.

Third: Understand what jealousy is.

The dictionary defines it as being:

- Fearful of losing what one has to another especially someone's love or affection.
- Resentful of others' success or advantage, etc.
- Arising from feelings of envy, apprehension, or bitterness.

Fourth: Go to God and ask for forgiveness. The Word says, **"If you confess your sin, He is faithful and just to forgive you your sin and cleanse you from all unrighteousness."** (1 John 1:9 paraphrased)

Once my understanding is clear on this, it is time to go on to the next step, healing.

This is defined as:
- To restore or return to health.
- To set right, amend, cure.

How do I go about doing this?

First: Recognize that only God can heal.

Second: Recognize that God wants to heal.

Third: Recognize that His Word has already provided healing; I Peter 2:24, Isaiah 53:5, and Psalm 91.

I realize that I can't control how others treat me, but I can control my response to it. The bible says, "Be angry but sin not: let not the sun go down upon your wrath; neither give place to the devil." Ephesians 4:26-27. I didn't respond well in the scenarios, my anger got the better of me and gave place to the devil which led to jealousy, but God taught me that following these steps will help me to overcome jealousy and envy. It will help me defeat the enemy, bring me closer to God, and remember that God wants His best for me, and He already provided it when He gave us His Son Jesus Christ. I will not let the tricks of the enemy keep me from enjoying God's best for me.

Chapter 4
DON'T MISS YOUR WINDOW OF OPPORTUNITY
2000
4.3

Numbers 13:1-33 is the story of the twelve spies that Moses sent to spy out the land of Canaan who came back and said that the land is full of milk and honey, but the people and the city were very great. There were only two who said the city could be taken but the other ten persuaded the Israelites not to go forward. This disobedience caused the anger of God to be kindled against them and He caused them to wander in the wilderness for 40 years.

Deuteronomy 1:20-21 tells how God brought them out of the wilderness into the land that He had promised them and how Joshua told the Children of Israel to go up and possess the land.

God has shown me how this is a window of opportunity that he wants me to see. The Children of Israel who were over 20 years old missed out on their window of opportunity because they did not believe God would give them the land and help them fight the people who were currently occupying it. God is preparing me to move into another level. He has selected a situation to push me into the next level, but if I murmur or complain like the Israelite's did, I will miss my window of opportunity. Will I walk in what God has designed for me or retreat to what is comfortable to me?

We can either accept it and walk in what God has prepared or reject it and walk in darkness and defeat. Just go get it; He has already made a way.

Chapter 4
OVERCOMING CONDEMNATION
February 11, 2002
4.4

God showed me today that Satan is trying to keep me in a spirit of condemnation to make me think I'm always doing something wrong, but God's Word says, **"There is therefore now no condemnation to them which are in Christ Jesus, who walk not after the flesh, but after the Spirit."** (Romans 8:1 KJV)

Therefore, I will not yield to the spirit of condemnation which would have me believe that God is not pleased with me or that He is always disappointed in me. I will walk in the knowledge that God loves me, that He created me in my mother's womb and gave me life, that He walks out my steps and leads me in the way everlasting.

Even though God might not like everything I do, just like parents, He loves me in spite of the things I do. When I ask for forgiveness, He forgives me, and we carry on.

Chapter 4
OVERCOMING FAULTS
March 17, 2002
4.5

Learning to overcome faults is not easy. While I was in prayer today, God told me to stop trying to overcome my faults by myself. If I could do it on my own, I would have done it a long time ago. He told me to trust **Him to perfect that which concerns me.** (Psalm 138:8 NKJV) He said to use the Word to overcome in these areas, find scripture to **call those things which be not as though they were** (Romans 4:17 NKJV), and repeat them every time. Do not worry that it sounds trite. The enemy is depending on me getting bored or tired of saying the same thing or thinking "this isn't working" so he can keep tempting me with it, but God says, "Say it every time: '**Submit yourself therefore to God. Resist the devil, and he will flee from you.**'" (James 4:7 NKJV) Use God's Word, for His Word has and is power. My words have no power. Stand on the promise of God.

Chapter 4
THE CLEAN UP
August 18, 2003
4.6

Have you ever seen someone who lives on the street and noticed how dirty they are? Their feet, ankles, elbows, and hands are all crusted over with dirt and even if they take a bath, the crusty dirt is still there. It takes more than one bath to get it all off. This is how sin is on our soul. Our soul is crusted over with the filth of sin, and after receiving salvation through the work of the Lord Jesus Christ on the cross, He sent the Holy Ghost to clean us up and bathe us with the Word of God.

God is in the process of bathing me and cleaning me up. Most of the surface dirt has been washed off; now we are addressing the crusty stuff, the things (dirt) that cling to me that must be scraped off, like around the ankle, knees, and elbows. They do not come off as easily and definitely not all in the first wash.

Some of these include attitude, sharp tongue, negative conversation, self-esteem (the way I see myself), arrogance, self-control, my conduct (I tend to fly off the handle), my desire to always be right, lack of patience, low attention span, and the desire to be like someone else.

Before negative character traits can be changed, they must first be recognized. You won't scrape your elbows clean if you don't recognize they're dirty. Sometimes you need to soak them a while to loosen the dirt before you can scrub it away. Which means sometimes we have to stay in our situation (soak) a while so that the Holy Ghost can loosen up the things He is trying to remove from us.

Ephesians 5:26 (NKJV) says, *"That He might sanctify and cleanse it [the church] with the washing of water by the Word."* The Holy Ghost is here to help us get ready to be presented before God. He is here to clean us up and get us dressed and ready to go with Jesus when He comes.

Chapter 4
UNREALISTIC DREAMS ABOUT MARRIAGE
December 31, 2003

4.7

It is the last day of the year, and I have read over the entries in my journal from throughout the year. Some of the revelations God has given me are utterly amazing. However, for a while now I have been dealing with bouts of depression until just recently. The depression stemmed from an incident of letting myself get excited over a very handsome man whom I inquired about from a friend and learned he was not married.

The excitement caused me to go to God to see what He thought and had to say concerning it. God said let it go and give up the dream. That crushed my heart and almost kept me from teaching one of the Sunday School lessons because it was about marriage, and it was too hard to give up my dream of getting married. My head said it was time to let go, but my heart was not ready for it.

Finally, after preparing my heart to let go, God helped me understand that He wasn't saying let go of the hope of getting married but let go of the dream. the (unrealistic expectation) that I had concerning marriage. There were too many delusions in my mind about what marriage should be like. It is exciting to know that God will help me gain the correct understanding of what marriage is actually about.

Chapter 4
WHAT FEAR HAS CAUSED
March 3, 2005
4.8

Last night on TV there was someone praying that people would be delivered from fear. I accepted that for myself and believe in my deliverance. This morning while reading James 2:20, which says **"...that faith without works is dead,"** it came to me that I must put work to my faith. Fear can cause so many problems and phobias. It can also cause stress-related health issues. The best way for me to overcome fear and put work to my faith is to acknowledge the things that fear has caused.

This is a list of the things that fear has kept me from or where it has hindered me.

- Fear has kept me from continuing in my decorating business.
- Fear has caused me to walk in pride which is a false sense of security.
- Fear has caused me to be afraid of the responsibility of success.
- Fear has kept me from trusting God.

Chapter 4
YEAR END REFLECTION
November 30, 2005
4.9

This morning was a time of reflection, thinking about the past year, what things were learned, what events have come to pass, and then relating it to what I am going through now. It seems I'm in the midst of turmoil.

At the beginning of the year, the Lord Jesus taught me about pride, covetousness, envy, and rebellion. He said He was putting me on an accelerated course. I learned that I was full of pride by learning what the components of pride are and how it affected my life. Sometime later in the year, the Lord allowed a wonderful man in my life but with that came rejection from some of my peers. It seems rejection is something I have dealt with all my life.

Many thoughts ran through my mind like "maybe becoming more like them would cause them to accept me." It worked while living in Los Angeles but after coming back home, nothing seemed to make a difference. I thought "maybe if they get to know me, they'll like me," the only problem was that participating in the things they did caused them to reject me even more. This brought me to the thought "maybe if they can see my artistic talent, they'll accept me," but that just made it even worse.

My mistake was trying to be like them, by starting to act like they did, it caused me to pick up some of their bad habits. It seems misery loves company. This attempt also failed and all it did was cause animosity and more rejection. Now when this should be the happiest time of my life, there's sorrow because of having to reap what I have sown. People are talking about me, putting me down, etc., but it is nobody's fault but my own. I planted many seeds of discord, backbiting, fault finding, and more, and it seems it was all in an effort to be accepted by the very people who are now finding fault with me. Well, the blessing is in knowing what the mistakes are so corrections can be made.

Earlier this year, the Lord Jesus also taught me about learning to be myself instead of hiding behind other people's masks (personality). Well, now I see where those masks have led me, **nowhere.** It is time to be me whether people like me or not.

God showed me that He keeps His promises by blessing me to meet a wonderful man. He fulfilled a dream of mine and made me realize that without Him my dreams mean nothing because He is the one who gave me my dreams. My dreams and goals will not be accomplished without Him, however *"I can do all things through Christ which strengthens me."* (Philippians 4:13 NKJV) He is God my Father.

REFLECTION

YOU WOULD RATHER DIE THAN LIVE WITHOUT ME

God is so good. There are many things that I have learned over the years, some things I already knew, but when they are put into a certain context or just worded a little differently, they seem to come to life in my heart and seems a lot clearer.

For about a two-week period, the Lord showed me several things. These are some of the things I learned.

- Stop trying to measure where I am in Christ with where other people are. I am not them. Strive to attain where God wants me to be and for my blessings, not seeking to receive what others have.

- The reason I am still going through the things I'm going through at work is because God does not intend to change the situation but to change me.

- The reason Satan keeps bringing up my past and trying to lay on me the quilt of my past is that he cannot control my future. God has given me precious promise for my future like Isaiah 54, Proverbs 31:10-31, Deuteronomy 28:1-14, Psalm 91. Isaiah 54 is a promise that I will forget the shame of my youth, so I must forget the past and keep focused on the future. Stop looking at the past and look at the promise.

- Do not say to myself, "I don't have the spirit of love in me," because God has put His Spirit in me, the Holy Ghost, so the spirit of love is already in me. I will ask God to help me develop the fruit of love. A seed must be planted before it will grow, and it takes time for the tree to grow before it produces fruit. It produces in its season, but even when it is not producing fruit the tree is still growing.

- What I will treasure the most is when you told me that You would rather die than live without me. Being that You already died for me and rose again, then that means You do not intend to live without me. You intend to make sure that I am with you throughout eternity. I love you Lord God.

Chapter 5

Introduction 5.1

GOD'S WISDOM KEYS

Wisdom keys are words of wisdom that God has given me over the years. Little tidbits of wisdom to help me overcome obstacles, make changes, correct habits, and help me see myself the way He sees me. They are keys that unlock doors of understanding. However, you must learn how to use the keys.

When you use a natural key, you put the key in the lock, and turn it to get the door to open. If you put the wrong key in, it will not turn the lock. Sometimes even if you put the right keys in you need to pull the door a little or push it in to get the tumblers in the right position so the key can turn. I have a drawer at work that has a key, and you have to push it in a little to get the key to turn. If you don't push the drawer in, although you have the right key, the key will not turn. So sometimes you might have the right key, but you still need to learn how to use it.

When God gives you a word of wisdom, find out where that word is to be applied. Is it your home life, work life, church life, or all the above? Most will be for all the above, but it might start out as a word for your work life, as an example, that can be applied everywhere. Learn how to use the key first in the area God is showing you, then you will be able to see how that same key will open doors in more areas of your life. These next pages are tailored to help you recognize God's wisdom keys and how they apply to you.

Also included in this chapter are word studies that break down words, by definition, that might help you see the scriptures a little differently. We will look at several words and see what they mean, how God sees them and how they can possibly be applied in your life.

Chapter 5

THIS IS NOT A FAIRY TALE

5.2

As a little girl, I grew up on fairy tales like Snow White, Sleeping Beauty, and Cinderella, and there were other stories like the Three Little Pigs, Little Red Riding Hood, and Goldilocks and the Three Bears. All these stories have an appeal to children, and they open up their imagination. Some stories, like Snow White, Sleeping Beauty, and Cinderella, have villains and heroes. The villain might be an evil stepmother, evil queen, or a big bad wolf. In many fairy tales, the hero is a handsome prince.

For a long time, I believed in fairy tales. I believed that my handsome prince was out there somewhere and one day would find me. Much of my time was filled with daydreams about how he would come and rescue me from some dangerous situation, and we would live happily ever after.

After many years of disappointment, I finally decided I did not believe in fairy tales anymore and decided to talk to God about it and said, "all fairy tales should be banned to keep little girls from suffering the same disappointment." God said, "wait a minute, I have a story I want to tell you."

"Once up on a time there was a beautiful princess who was locked in a huge tower with no way out and it was guarded by an evil dragon. The princess was his slave and had to do whatever the evil dragon said do. The great and mighty king knew of the plight of the beautiful princess and sent His only Son the handsome prince to rescue her. When the prince saw the princess, He fell in love and knew He had to rescue her from the evil dragon. When He saw the dragon, He realized there was only one way to defeat him. He fought the dragon. The dragon was quite powerful and killed the handsome prince. Oh, what a day. The princess thought all was lost.

"As a victory celebration, the dragon tormented the princess even more. But what the dragon did not know is that before the prince fought the dragon, the king had given Him a special Holy ointment that would prevent any weapon used against the prince from lasting for more than three days, even the weapon of death. So, after three days the prince rose from the dead with all power in His hands, and He rescued the princess from the tower, destroyed the dragon, and took the princess to live with Him forever and they lived happily ever after."

Just in case you didn't get it, but I know you did, the princess is you and I (the world). The tower we were locked in is sin, and the dragon is Satan. The mighty king is God the Father, the holy ointment is the Holy Ghost, and the handsome prince is Christ Jesus himself.

While I was waiting for a handsome prince to come and rescue me, God showed me that Christ Jesus had already done it over 2,000 years ago on the cross and is in heaven now preparing a place for me (and you) for when he comes back to get me.

This is way more powerful than a fairy tale and the fact is, it is a true story, not make believe. We can believe it because it already happened. Christ already came, already died and rose from the dead, and already assured our place in heaven. All we need to do is accept Him as payment for our sins, then we are to live holy lives through the anointing of the Holy Ghost as we wait for his return. Isn't that wonderful? This is not a fairy tale, but God's own story told by God Himself.

Chapter 5

FOUR KEYS TO ANSWERED PRAYER

5.3

1. Know what you want from God and be specific.

2. Get your Bible and research to find scriptures that pertain to your situation.

3. Ask God for what you want (Matthew 7:8), be patient and wait on God. When you ask, you will get an answer from God – but in His time and according to His will. However, do not be disappointed if God says "no"; it might be that He has something better in mind for you.

4. Believe that you will receive what you are asking for. (Mark 11:23-24)

Chapter 5
GIFTS THAT GOD WANTS TO GIVE US
5.4

The Lord will sometimes put things into our hearts to ask Him for in prayer. They are giftings that God wants to give us and the way we receive them is by asking Him for them and believing by faith that we receive them. When you give someone a gift, your hope is that they receive it with joy and that it is something they will like. So, what God does is drop the thought into your mind of something He would like to give you. When you think about it, you might say to yourself, "that sounds good, that's what I think I want," then you go out and get it. What God wants us to do is ask Him for it, then when it comes to pass, we appreciate the gift God has given us.

An example would be when we are young, and God wants to lead us in our career choice. He might drop a thought in your mind that you want to be a doctor, an engineer, a teacher, or a business owner. When we seek God for it, He will help make sure you reach your goal because it is what He wants for you. Another example could be if He wanted you to have a certain kind of car, a house, a husband, or children. He will put it in your mind to ask Him for it, and He will help you to get it.

The scripture says, *"Every good gift and every perfect gift is from above, and comes down from the Father of lights, with whom is no variableness, neither shadow of turning."* (James 1:17 KJV) Sadly, many times God puts something in our hearts to ask for, and we try to go out on our own and get it without asking Him. God knows how to give good gifts to His children. If He wants you to have it, He knows how to make sure you get it. But He wants us to wait for Him to give it to us, not go get it ourselves.

So the next time you have a thought about something you want, realize that the thought might be a gift that God wants to give you and seek Him for it and receive it by faith. If the thought is from Him, He will make sure you receive it. Many times, it will come by special means like a reduced price or no down payment or someone might give it to you free. You might find favor in a certain situation. God might perform a miracle for you. There are many ways He might use to give you the gift He wants you to have.

The greatest gift He wants us to have is Salvation through Jesus Christ. He draws us to himself. So many people say, "I found Jesus," but actually He pursued you and put the thought in your mind to want Him and when you repent and surrender to Him you receive the greatest gift of all, Eternal life. Many people think they can get Eternal life through other means, but you can only get it the way God Himself set it up. You cannot get it on your own. You have to do it the way the Creator designed it. There is no other way because there is no other God.

Chapter 5
DON'T LET THE GIANTS STOP YOU
1999
5.5

God has seen your suffering. He has something better for you, but you have to stop looking back in Egypt (your past). The same God that brought you out of Egypt can keep you out until He gets you where He's taking you. God is greater than obstacles, like Satan telling you that you cannot get what God has for you or you'll never be what He wants you to be. If you heard God say, "Do not let Satan hinder you," then stand on what He said. God is a giant killer. If you hold on, God will make you a giant killer too, like in the story of David and Goliath. (1 Samuel 17:33-50)

Chapter 5
QUESTIONS TO ASK YOURSELF
1999
5.6

So often we as people are too focused on what is going on in the world — and rightly so because there is quite a lot going on. But too often our focus ends up turning to what everyone else is doing, and many times we end up gossiping, backbiting, and giving our opinion on what somebody else should be doing. Unfortunately, we do not always look at ourselves to see what we should do. Here are some questions we can ask ourselves to help us stay focused on what God would have us to do so we can stay out of other people's business.

Focus on these questions each day:
- How can I be of help to someone else?
- What in my life can I change so that others can see the Christ in me?
- How far am I willing to go to help others?
- Would God be pleased with my life today?

As you evaluate your life, ask these questions:

- Is this working?
- Are others benefiting from my life?
- Is God pleased with me?

Chapter 5
READ THE WORD, USE THE WORD, DO THE WORD
August 9, 1999
5.7

It is amazing how God helps me recognize things I need to do. Today He is showing me that I need to read the Word more, use the Word to overcome situations and obstacles, and do the Word to change my life.

- When I **<u>Read</u>** the Word, God gives me understanding of what He wants to do in my life and what He wants to change.

- When I **<u>Use</u>** the Word, I can overcome the enemy and the snares he puts in my life. I can make things happen and prevent things from happening.

- When I **<u>Do</u>** the Word, I put what I have learned into practical application (put it to use in my life) to become a ***doer of the Word and not a hearer only.*** (James 1:22)

Chapter 5
DON'T TELL THEM YOUR SECRETS
2000
5.8

God has an amazing journey planned for your life that he wants to tell you about. A plan just for you and no one else. As He tells you His plan, you need to be careful to guard it as David did when he was anointed to be king by Samuel then went back to tending the sheep. (1 Samuel 16:1-13) He didn't reveal God's plan for his life to anyone; only his family knew. He guarded this secret plan and watched God bring it to pass.

Guarding God's plan for you is important because not everyone who calls themselves your friends are people you can trust. Some people will use your secrets against you to destroy you. This was the case with Samson in Judges 16:1-5, 15-20. He put his trust in Delilah and told her his most precious secret, and she used it to betray him. Another example is Joseph. He told his brothers the dream God gave him, and it fueled their already jealous hearts against him, which led them to throw him in a pit with the intent to kill him. Instead, they decided to sell him for money — and this was his family! (Genesis 37:2-36)

Ask God to show you whom you can trust. But even in that, there are some things you just have to keep between you and God. Some things you have to wait until they manifest before you can tell anyone about them, or they might not come to pass. There are some things that God will do against the norm that people will try to talk you out of, saying that isn't God.

If you know for sure God told you something, keep it to yourself. You can write it down and date it so that when it comes to pass you have proof of what was said and when. You can also ask God if you are allowed to share it with anyone and only tell those whom He says it is all right to tell because they can sometimes be a witness of what God has said. After it has manifested, then you can tell it to others because now it is a testimony to the world.

Chapter 5
OCCUPY TIL I COME
2000

5.9

It's amazing how one word can mean so much, and because words are so important, God wrapped the Word in flesh and called His name Jesus. Jesus chose His words carefully and spoke many parables to make the Word understandable to men.

One day, God had me read the parable in Luke 19:13 then he had me look up one word that stood out, the word "occupy." After I wrote down the definition of the word, the Lord gave me a revelation about the scripture that gave me a better understanding of what we as the saints of God are supposed to be doing until Christ returns.

LUKE 19:13

OCCUPY — definition:
- To *seize possession* of and maintain control over a place or region.
- To *fill or take* time or space.
- To *dwell or reside* in.

- To *hold or fill* an office.
- To *engage* or busy oneself.

Let us review what the parable says.

Luke 19:11-27 says, "He said therefore, 'A certain nobleman went into a far country to receive for himself a kingdom, and to return. And he called his ten servants, and delivered them ten pounds, and said to them, <u>Occupy till I come</u>. But his citizens hated him, and sent a message after him, saying, We will not have this man to reign over us.

And it came to pass, that when he was returned, having received the kingdom, then he commanded these servants to be called unto him, to whom he had given the money, that he might know how much every man had gained by trading.

Then came the first, saying, Lord, thy pound hath gained ten pounds. And he said unto him, Well, thou good servant: because thou has been faithful in a very little, have thou authority over ten cities.

And the second came, saying, Lord, thy pound hath gained five pounds. And he said likewise to him, Be thou also over five cities.

And another came, saying, Lord behold, here is thy pound, which I have kept laid up in a napkin: For I feared thee, because thou art an austere man: thou takest up that thou layedst not down, and reapest where thou didst not sow. And he saith unto him, Out of thine own mouth will I judge thee, thou wicked servant. Thou knewest that I was an austere man, taking up that I laid not down, and reaping that I did not sow: Wherefore then *gavest not thou my money into the bank, that at my coming I might have required mine own with usury?*

And he said unto them that stood by, Take from him the pound, and give it to him that hath ten pounds. (And they said unto him, Lord, he hath ten pounds.) For I say unto you, That unto every one which hath shall be given; and from him that hath not, even that he hath shall be taken away from him. But those mine enemies, which would not that I should reign over them, bring hither, and slay them before me." (KJV)

Now let's break it down:

One version of the Bible (NKJV) says, "Do Business till I come," however I believe this misses the whole point. The parable talks of a nobleman (which is Jesus), who went to a far country (which is Earth), to receive for Himself a kingdom (which is the church). He called his servants (which are you and I) and gave them 10 commandments. He told them:

- I have given you authority (power over the enemy) to *Seize Possession* of the land and maintain control over it till I come back again.
- You should *Take Time* to help those who are in need. Love your enemies, bless those that curse you, love your neighbor as yourself, set the captives free, give sight to the blind, make

the lame walk, and make disciples of many.
- While you *Dwell and Reside* here, remember that you are *in* the world, not *of* the world. heaven is your home.
- You *Hold and Fill* the office of ambassador for Christ.
- So, *Engage and keep yourself busy being* about your Father's business.

<u>Be the light of the world</u>. (Matthew 5:14a)

<u>Be the city that is set on a hill that cannot be hid</u>. (Matthew 5:14b)

<u>Be the light on a lamp stand that gives light to all who are in the house</u>. (Matthew 5:15b)

"Let your light shine before men, that they may see your good work, and glorify your Father which is in heaven." (Matthew 5:16)

This is how the saints of God are to "Occupy till He comes" and fulfill the true meaning of this one word.

Chapter 5
SIN
2003
5.10

Self - Indulgence - Neurosis

While I was in prayer one day God gave me a revelation on the meaning of the word "SIN."

- SELF — The total being of one person. The Individual. One's own interest, welfare, or advantage.
- INDULGENCE — Indulge: to yield to the desires or will of, pamper, to gratify; satisfy. To allow oneself a special pleasure.
    (SELF-INDULGENCE: Excessive indulgence of one's own appetites and desires.)
- NEUROSIS — A disorder in which the function of the mind or emotions is disturbed with no apparent physical cause.

This tells us that sin causes a disorder of the mind that causes excessive indulgence of one's own appetites and desires. Sin is a selfish act with no concern for others. This is where lying, cheating, murder, rape, drug use and addiction, adultery, fornication, idolatry, witchcraft, sexual immorality, jealousy, and covetousness comes from. However, when you Humble yourself before God, confess that you are a sinner and accept His Son Christ Jesus as your Savior and Lord, God will forgive you of your sin and cleanse you from all unrighteousness.

This acronym can help keep things in prospective:

H — Him first

U — you second

M — me third

B — both of us fourth

L — lots of us fifth

E — every one of us sixth

This will keep your focus in the right place and help you avoid SIN.

Chapter 5
FRUIT OF THE SPIRIT
March 8, 2004
5.11

When Jesus lived on earth, He was one man living in one body on earth who could only be in one place at a time. Through His death and resurrection, He is able to live His perfect life on earth through us. He lives on the inside of us and lives His holy life through us by the Holy Ghost. But we need to allow Him to do so. The Fruit of the Spirit (Galatians 5:22-23) is also born out of Love and we know God is Love so we are going to look at the Fruit from two aspects, Death and Love.

When Paul said, "I die daily" (1 Corinthians 15:31), he is saying "I die to myself so that Christ might live in and through me." So, we need to die to the things that are not like Christ in order for Him to live His life through us. What do we die to?

- We must die to sin so that His *Love* might reign through us.
- We must die to anger so His *Joy* (Christ's Strength) might live through us.
- We must die to envy and jealousy, wrath, and anxiety

so His *Peace* (<u>Christ's Security</u>) might live though us.
- We must die to impatience so that His *Longsuffering* (<u>Christ's Patience</u>) can live through us.
- We must die to our bad attitude, unkindness, gossip, and slander so that His *Gentleness* (<u>Christ's Conduct</u>) can live through us.
- We must die to rejoicing over the failure of others and praising people who do wicked things and let His *Goodness* (<u>Christ's Character</u>) live though us.
- We must die to doubt and unbelief and let His *Faith* (<u>Christ's Confidence</u>) live through us.
- We must die to pride and arrogance so that His *Meekness* (<u>Christ's Humility</u>) can live through us.
- We must die to rude behavior, selfishness, evil thinking, being easily provoked so that His *Temperance — Self-control* (<u>Christ's Victory</u>) can live through us.

When we die to the flesh, then Christ's Spirit (Fruit) can live through us.

Now let's look at the Fruit of the Spirit through the eyes of <u>Love</u>.
1 Corinthians 13:4-8a

"Love" is defined in the dictionary as "Intense affection or warm feeling for another, a strong fondness or enthusiasm, a beloved person (dearly loved). A strong desire for another person."

The scriptures use the word "Charity" for the word "Love" and is defined in the dictionary as "Help or alms (money or goods) given to the poor, an organization or fund that helps the poor, an act or feeling of benevolence, forbearance in judging others (forbearance = to refrain or desist from, to be tolerant of, patient) – the benevolence of God toward man – goodwill or brotherly love.

Charity is more than giving to the poor and love is more than just a feeling. Both have a conduct and a character and many other attributes. This is how we as the Saints of God should love one another.

- Love is *Patient* with others and <u>Suffers</u> a <u>Long</u> time with them.
- Love's *Conduct* is *Gentle* enough to be <u>Kind</u> to everyone it meets even to its enemies.
- Love is *Secure* enough to be at *Peace,* so it has no reason to <u>Envy</u>.
- Love is *Humble* enough to be *Meek* therefore it does <u>not *Parade*</u> itself and is <u>not *Puffed up*</u> or Arrogant.
- Love has enough *Self-control* that it does <u>not *Behave*</u>

Rudely, is not _Easily Provoked_, is not _Selfish_, does not _Think Evil_ thoughts.

- Love has a *Character* of **Goodness** and does not take joy in Wickedness or Sinfulness but takes Joy in Truth.
- Love has the *Confidence* of **Faith** to _Bear All Things, Believe All Things, and Hope All Things._

- Love has the *Strength* of **Joy** to _Endure All Things_, therefore it **Never Fails**.

When we conduct ourselves with these characteristics, we can fulfill the commandment of Jesus to love God and to love our neighbors as ourselves but remember that we have the Holy Spirit to live these characteristics through us. We do not have to rely on our own power to do it.

Chapter 5
DARKNESS BEFORE THE LIGHT
2005
5.12

Genesis 1:2 (NKJV) says, "And the earth was without form and void; and darkness was upon the face of the deep. And the Spirit of God moved upon the face of the waters." This passage is talking about how the earth began in darkness and the Spirit of God moved in the midst of that darkness. While it was yet dark, He moved upon the face of the water. Do you wonder how God can work in the dark? Psalm 139:12 says darkness and light are both alike to Him.

In verses 3-5 of Genesis, it talks about, how when God spoke, something happened, something changed, there was now light, and He divided them and gave them names. He called the light "day" and the darkness He called "night." The most fascinating thing about this verse is that it says, "the evening and the morning were the first day." Notice that the day did not start with the light, it started in darkness then came the light. In verses 8, 13, 19, 23 and 31, it says, "the evening and the morning were the first, second, all the way to the sixth day. What does this tell us? Evening comes before morning, night comes before day, darkness comes before light, and tribulation comes before triumph.

It might be dark in your life right now, but that does not mean that God is not working. Some of His best work was done in the dark. When God split the Red Sea, it was at night (Exodus 14:19-25). Also, we see it in the life of some of God's people like Joseph who went through much tribulation (darkness) - night, before he became second in command of Egypt, his triumph (day) - light. David went through a long period of darkness (night) - before the day he became king.

We also see it in life itself. Babies are formed in the darkness of the womb and then birthed into light. While they are in the womb, they are being formed, shaped, and prepared to face the wonders that life has in store for them. God sets a plan for that life. No one is here by accident.

While we are going through tribulation, we are being formed, shaped, and prepared for the blessings that God has for us. Do not despise the darkness, because that is when God is moving in our lives, removing things like habits, attitudes, ways, and strongholds while bringing new things to light like patience, strength, joy, peace, and love.

Genesis verses 1 and 2 say, "In the beginning God created…" (you were created by God) "…and the earth was without form and void," which means it was nothing. It had no life, no shape; it was just a lump of nothing. But then God's Spirit moved upon it and He brought life to it. Our life before Christ is nothing, no life, no shape, then God's Spirit moves upon us when we accept Christ Jesus as our Lord and Savior, and He says let there be light. John 1: 1-13 talks about the Word, Jesus, being that light.

Now Jesus is the Word and in Him is life and the life is the light of men. The Light shined in the darkness of your life and you began to see things that were stuffed in corners, hidden in closets, and stuffed behind the doors of your life, etc., things you forgot were there or wanted to keep hidden. Then He begins to clean house and bring in new things. Notice when He created the earth, He didn't leave it dark, He turned on the light and brought in flowers, trees, birds, grass, herbs, fruit, fish, and more animals. He brought in beautiful things.

When He turns on the light in our lives and cleans our spiritual house, then He begins to bring in the beautiful things like faith, hope, and love, the beauty of holiness, righteousness, and fellowship with Him. All these things are first formed in the darkness of tribulation then brought to the light of triumph.

Chapter 5
RESPECT vs. PRIDE
January 10, 2005
5.13

The wisdom of God is amazing, and He is willing to share His wisdom with us and help us learn how to use His Wisdom Keys. The following is wisdom from God concerning the difference between respect and pride.

The definition of "respect" is deference or high regard, esteem — to have esteem for, to avoid violation of, to concern.

Deferential = deference — courteous submission to the opinion, wishes or judgment of another, courteous respect.

Esteem = to place high value on, prize, to judge to be, consider, favorable regard as in Proverbs 31:10.

The definition of "pride" includes conceit, arrogance. To indulge in self-esteem, glory.

This morning Jesus said to me, "I placed high value on you when I died for you. You were worth my life. You are precious in my sight. You are worth more than pride can offer you. Pride offers a false sense of security. Respect offers a true sense of worth."

Have respect for yourself, not pride in yourself. Proverb 21:4 says, "A high look, and a proud heart, and the plowing of the wicked, is sin." (Webster's Bible Translation) Proverb 16:18-19 says "Pride goeth before destruction, and a haughty spirit before a fall. Better it is to be of an humble spirit with the lowly, than to divide the spoil with the proud." (KJV)

Chapter 5
COMMIT THY WAY UNTO THE LORD
June 12, 2005
5.14

Psalm 37:5 says, "Commit thy way unto the Lord; trust also in Him; and He shall bring it to pass." (KJV)

The word <u>Commit</u> means to consign, entrust, to place in confinement or custody.

The word <u>Consign</u> means to give over to the care of another, entrust.

I always thought the phrase "commit your way," meant to make a decision to follow the Lord in all your ways. To do something, perform or promise something. It really means give your ways over to the care of God.

The word <u>Way</u> means a manner of doing something, a method or technique, a habit, characteristic, or tendency. A customary course of action or state of affairs.

In other words, give your manner of doing things, your habits, or tendency over to the care of God. Place them in His custody for safe keeping.

REST IN THE LORD

"Rest in the Lord, and wait patiently for Him." Psalm 37:7a

The word <u>Rest</u> means a period of inactivity, relaxation, or sleep. Absence of activity or motion. To refresh oneself. To become or remain temporarily quiet or inactive. To depend or rely on.

Learn to take time to rest in the Lord. Get quiet before Him, relax in Him. Learn to depend and rely on Him.

Chapter 5
THE WHOLE ARMOR OF GOD
2007
5.15

Ephesians 6: 10-17

Ephesians 6:10 says, "Finally, my brethren, be strong in the Lord, and in the power of His might." (NKJV)
One day while I was praying, God gave me an amazing revelation on being strong in the Lord and the "Whole Armor of God." First, he had me start with verse 10 and made me realize that I need an understanding of the words, so he had me look up the words "strong," "power," and "might."

- Strong = physically powerful, muscular, in good sound health, robust. Capable of enduring stress or strain. Intense in degree or quality. Forceful or persuasive. Extreme, drastic.
- Power = the ability of capacity to act or perform effectively. A specified capacity, faculty, or aptitude (had the power of concentration) strength or force. Capable of being exerted, might. The ability or capacity to exercise control or authority. One having influence or control over another. Physical strength.

- Might = the power to resist or sustain and attack, moral courage or power. Effective or binding force, the power to resist force, stress, or strain. Toughness.

Once I understood the meaning of the words, He showed me how to put them together differently to get a better understanding of the verse.

- We are to be (strong) in good sound health, capable of enduring stress or strain. We are to be forceful or persuasive when necessary (we have to force our flesh to give in to His spirit).
- We are to be strong in the Lord (and in the power of His might). His ability to perform effectively, His ability to exercise control, His authority, His ability to influence and control others. His ability to resist or sustain an attack, His moral courage. His ability to keep you intact.

This means trusting in God's abilities, not our own.

- Trust = firm reliance, confident belief, one in whom confidence is placed, one committed into the care of another. Reliance on something in the future, hope. To expect with assurance, to believe, to entrust.

In other words, we are to have firm reliance in God's ability and commit (entrust) ourselves into His care and to expect with assurance that He is able to perform effectively.

Now let's look at the Whole Armor of God

When we put on the armor of God, we are not putting on God's armor as if it is pieces of a garment. We are actually putting on God Himself. When you look at this scripture you notice that all the pieces of armor are characteristics of God. We are to have our loins girded about with truth, have on the breastplate of righteousness, our feet shod with the preparation of gospel of peace, above all taking the shield of faith, and the helmet of salvation and the sword of the spirit, which is the Word of God. So that makes Jesus our truth, our righteousness, our peace; our faith is in Him; He is our salvation; and He (the Word) is our sword of the spirit, our weapon, making God our full covering of protection and our weapon of warfare.

REFLECTION

THE POTTER'S HOUSE
Jeremiah 18:1-6

The art of pottery is a beautiful art form. It requires skill and creativity to make a beautiful and functional piece of pottery, also known as ceramics. There are four essential elements needed for pottery: earth, water, fire, and one other essential element. You must have all these elements together. The water changes the earth to make it into clay, which is formed into a vessel that is transformed by fire into a functional piece of pottery. This is all done by the fourth essential element — the potter, without which none of the other elements can come together. Isaiah 64:8 says, "But now, O Lord, thou art our Father; we are the clay, and thou our potter; and we all are the work of thy hand." (KJV)

When a potter makes a vessel, the hands and spirit of the potter transform every piece into a work of art. The final firing gives life to each creation. The clay has no form of its own. Its task is to offer infinite possibilities. So it is with God. He is the potter; we are the clay. He transforms us into a vessel individually designed and created by the hand of God. No two people are just alike, not even twins. We all have different shapes, colors, personalities, and gifts, offering infinite possibilities.

There are three stages to pottery making:
1. Stage one is shaping and molding.
2. Stage two is drying.
3. Stage three is firing.

We are going to go through each stage carefully because each stage is especially important.

Stage 1 – Shaping and molding: Clay is an inorganic substance that when mixed with water makes a workable substance that can be shaped and molded into various objects. The clay is put on a wheel and shaped by hand as the wheel spins around. The potter must apply water several times throughout the molding process to keep the clay malleable, which means "capable of being shaped or formed" and keeps it from drying out.

As the wheel spins, the clay begins to take shape. The potter shapes the walls and the bottom of the vessel. Each time the wheel goes around the vessel, walls go higher and higher and it begins to take shape however the potter sees fit. The clay has no say so in what it becomes; only the potter knows what it will be made into. The clay cannot say to the potter, "I want to be a teapot" or "I want to be a vase." Only the potter can say what the clay will become. Isaiah 45:9 says, "Woe unto him that striveth with his Maker! Let the potsherd strive with the potsherds of the earth. Shall the clay say to him that fashioneth it, What makest thou? or thy work, He hath no hands?" (KJV)

Romans 9:20-21 says, "Nay but, O man, who art thou that repliest against God? Shall the thing formed say to him that formed it, Why hast thou made me thus? Hath not the potter power over the clay, of the same lump to make one vessel unto honour and another unto dishonour?" (KJV) When we are born again, God begins shaping us and molding us into what he wants us to become. He has a design already in mind before we are even born.

During the molding and shaping process, it is particularly important that the clay stay moist to keep it malleable (capable of being shaped and molded). To do this, the potter's hands must stay wet, so he will dip them in water at various times and apply it to the clay to keep the clay wet. The water that God applies to us comes in the form of spiritual rain. Some rain comes through small spring showers (small tests we might go through). This is also when God rains showers of blessings on us. Everything is going well, we are growing and learning to use our faith (the reason for the small test), seeing God move mightily in our lives. We are so excited about being saved during this time, and this is the time when we want to tell everyone we know about God.

Then there are other types of rain that come through the thunderstorms (those storms of life that blow through our lives). They are dark and gloomy and full of clouds and heavy winds that knock things over and sometimes tear things apart. As each storm passes, God uses the water of that storm to continue to shape us into the vessel He has designed us to be.

As you're standing on the wheel (the Word of God), the wheel goes around, and around, and around, and the walls of the vessel get higher and higher. This means your faith gets stronger and stronger because you are standing on the wheel (the Word of God) which says, "So then faith comes by hearing [and hearing and hearing...], and hearing by the Word of God." (Romans 10:17 NKJV) So the turning of the wheel is the turning of the Word of God over and over in our hearts and minds, making your faith stronger and stronger. You begin hearing words like, "I will never leave you nor forsake you." Hebrews 13:5 (NKJV) "I will be with him in trouble; I will deliver him and honor him." Psalm 91:15 (NKJV) "Therefore do not be like them, for your Father knows the things you have need of before you ask Him." Matthew 6:8 (NKJV) "Being confident of this very thing, that He which hath begun a good work in you will perform it until the day of Jesus Christ." Philippians 1:6 (KJV)

So, when the storms of life start raging remember that with

the storm comes rain and with the rain comes growth just like the rain that comes down from heaven and waters the earth and causes the flowers to bloom, the grass to grow and the trees to yield their fruit. These storms are the test and trials that God uses to begin separating us from the world. When your friends don't treat you the way they used to and your family begins to ostracize you and your co-workers persecute you, these are the storms that shape your life and determine what kind of person or vessel that you will be and begin to prepare you for the next stage of the process which is drying.

Stage 2 — Drying: This is where the vessel has been shaped and formed into the design the potter had in mind and is now ready to be removed from the wheel and is set out to dry. There are several stages in the drying process that take it from being malleable to a harder stage where it can be handled without fear of deforming the shape, but different decorative touches can be added like handles, spouts or attachments. At this stage alterations can be made if necessary.

This stage is also where burnishing can be done. Burnishing is where the clay is made smooth by rubbing it with a hard object like a stone which gives the piece a polished look and removes any excess clay. As we go through our drying process, we might find ourselves alone. Our friends are far and few in between. We try to reach out to people, but no one seems to be there. We begin to feel all alone. This is an extremely important time. It is the time when God wants to spend time with us Himself by separating us from others so He can smooth out the rough spots and give us a good polish. He wants us to seek Him out, to look for Him. This is the time when many people fall because they do not understand what process they are in. If you go through the process correctly, you will understand that this is your time alone with God. This is the time when God can add decorative features such as gifts of the Spirit, knowledge, understanding, wisdom, and more (the smoothing). You are beginning to learn the Word of God and put it into action (the polishing).

But if we don't go through the process correctly, it will cause problems. We must be careful and remember the scripture that says, "...Be not weary in well doing..." (2 Thessalonians 3:13 KJV), because many of us at this stage get lax; we get frustrated and can become marred; we go back to old ways and bad habits because we feel alone. This is sometimes where people make mistakes like calling up old boyfriends or girlfriends or going to old hang outs and do things they regret later, and the potter has to put us back on the wheel and start all over again. When you go through the drying process the right way and the drying process is complete, there is very little moisture left, and you have overcome the storms that used to cause you problems, like being ostracized by friends, criticism from people about your salvation, or loneliness (you look forward to being alone with God). The vessel is now ready for the final stage of the process — the fire.

Stage 3 — Firing: The vessel must be as dry as possible before going into the fire or the clay might explode as it heats in what is called the kiln, the oven in which the pottery is placed into for firing. During the firing process, the clay goes through a transformation whereby it is fused together into a solid piece and is permanently changed. Prior to the transformation, when the clay objects are reintroduced to water, the clay particles will fall apart and re-dissolve into the water. They can then be re-constituted into workable clay. After firing, the clay becomes impervious to water. Some pieces are put through the fire several times to achieve the potter's desired results. Higher fired clays are more durable than others.

Now do not be afraid to go through the fire because God has promised to be with you in the fire. Isaiah 43:2 (KJV) says, "When thou passest through the waters, I will be with thee; and through the rivers, they shall not overflow thee: when thou walkest through the fire, thou shalt not be burned, neither shall the flame kindle upon thee."

We have a particularly good example of this in Daniel chapter 3 when Shadrach, Meshach, and Abednego were literally thrown into a burning, fiery furnace. Now fire can either destroy you as it did the men who delivered them to the entrance of the furnace, or it can forever change you. You might remember in the story how the king saw a fourth man in the fire and said, "the form of the fourth is like the Son of God." (Daniel 3:25 KJV) Now all these men were walking around in the fire unharmed. The rope that had them bound burned off, but the clothes they were wearing, the shoes they had on, the hats and their very person were untouched. The fire didn't burn them or even scorch the hair on their heads; however, their lives were never the same. The king acknowledged their God as the true and living God and promoted them to high ranks in this kingdom.

Once God has molded and shaped you and brought you through the fire, you have become a beautiful vessel that can be used for God's glory at His command for whatever he desires. No longer are you a lump of clay but a beautiful vessel "meet for the Master's use" (2 Timothy 2:21 KJV) – but be careful; don't get high minded, because a beautiful vessel can easily become dysfunctional or broken.

A functional vessel has a purpose for which it was created like a teapot, bowl, mugs, or vases, etc. Some items are created strictly for decorations like sculptures or wall hangings. God made us to be functional vessels He can use, but sometimes we get out of His will and become dysfunctional. Here is an example: I have two pair of scissors; both have the same purpose. They are both designed the same and shaped the same and are both made to cut things. One pair is functional because they are sharp and straight and will cut anything I choose to use them on. The other pair, however, is not functional because it is dull and warped and will not cut most things except paper — maybe. I can't use them for most of the things I need them for and will eventually discard them.

I also have two can openers: one is electric, and the other is manual. The electric one has a beautiful design and looks pretty sitting on the counter, but it malfunctions 80% of the time. While the manual one is by no means pretty, but it functions 100% of the time, it is harder to use but at least it works.

Are you a vessel that is functional and meet for the Master's use or are you a vessel that malfunctions and is set aside to be discarded? Do you look good but do not operate in the capacity for which you were created, or are you always available for use? Have you been marred in the potter's hand? Well remember if you are honest with yourself and with God and humble yourself under His hand, He can remake you into a functional vessel that is meet for His use.

Because we are people and are made from the earth, we are ripe for making into clay. We might go through the process of being put on the wheel several time in our lives and being made over and over again. Because we are a spirit that lives in a physical body and have a soul, our physical bodies are not remade but our soul is. Each time we are put on the wheel, molded, shaped, put on the shelf for the drying time and then put through the fire, we are permanently changed. We are stronger than we were before, we are wiser than we were before. The way we think is transformed and the way we act is conformed, by the Master's hand over and over again until we are made into the image of Christ by the Holy Ghost.

Chapter 6

Introduction 6.1

PROPHECIES FROM THE LORD GOD

2005

This chapter contains prophecies God has given me about my life and other things. Some have been fulfilled, and others are in the process of being fulfilled. I included them in the book because they have helped me see where God is taking me.

You might have prophecies in your life that either God told you Himself or were spoken to you by a prophet during a revival or another service. If you do, write them down and date them and when they come to pass, go back and write the dates they were fulfilled.

As I mentioned, some of mine have come to pass and I have dated them and told how they were fulfilled. Others are being fulfilled as I write, and some are still to be completed but are in the process of fulfillment.

Chapter 6
PROPHECY
1995
6.2

Beware of him who comes before me with pleasant word and conversation and good looks for he is not the one sent to me. He only comes to distract and destroy me, for with him comes much pain and heartbreak he will be good to look at but in him is darkness.

After that will come sorrow and grief to those around me, and my strength in the Lord will comfort them. Do not be distracted by the grief, for it is only designed to distract me and to try to cause me to give up. Be patient and strong in the Lord, for it will only last a minute. After that will come much joy and rejoicing in God the Father.

UPDATE

This prophecy was fulfilled in the year 1999 and 2000; I met a man whom I thought was the one for me. He was in the church, and we got along so well, but it did not last. He became interested in someone else in the church and it caused me a lot of pain, more than I had ever experienced before. The reason it hurt so bad was he represented all the men in my life who had previously rejected me. God told me to let go but I couldn't, and I asked the Lord to help me let go. He helped me, but the process was very painful. However, I also learned an extremely valuable lesson in forgiveness.

About a year later, our church experienced a split when the pastor of the church at that time walked out and took half of the congregation with him. Just before he left, our church went through a very painful experience. There were a lot of accusations, lies, and betrayal. It took about a year for us to recover. We humbled ourselves before God and He healed us. In the year 2001 we were blessed with a new pastor, and we have been rejoicing ever since. Our church is now growing. We were left with about 40 or so people and now our church is full, and we are in the process of plans to build a new facility. Many who left have returned and so have several families that had left way before it all started. The Lord is so faithful.

Chapter 6
PRAY FOR YOURSELF
2003
6.3
A WORD FROM THE LORD

One day in prayer God told me that I do not pray enough for myself. God said, "you have to pray that you will do the right things in your day. Pray for yourself that you will give soft answers that turn away wrath, that you will be quick to listen – people are telling you something behind the words they say, but you are not hearing them. Pray that you will make the right choices. Pray that you will have a listening ear to hear from God. Pray that you will have a determined mind to do whatever He says."

God is saying, "I am going to make you perfect in all you do. The way you are at work, at church, at home, and in relationships with family and friends, I am going to make you perfect so you can see what perfection is like. Not that you yourself are perfect but having a perfect relationship with God will allow Me to perfect everything in your life. You will learn what perfection in Christ is really like. Don't be afraid of what you see or hear; just rejoice in God."

Chapter 6
DELIGHT
November 29, 2004
6.4

Yesterday during prayer at church, in the prayer line, my pastor spoke a word over me. He said, "God says, 'Delight yourself in the Lord' (Psalm 37:4); you've been believing God for something special and He says, 'Delight yourself in Me then shall you know My thoughts, and My thoughts will be your thoughts.' Then He will give you the desire of your heart. 'No good thing will I withhold from you.'"

That is the gist of what he said. It might not be verbatim, but this is not the first time He spoke this to me. The first time He spoke this was on my birthday. God had already blessed me but urged me to go up front for prayer. When I went, the pastor prayed and said, "God says, 'before you ask, I will answer.' He said, 'Delight yourself in the Lord and He will give you the desire of your heart.' God says, 'You wonder if it is too late,' but God says, 'It is not too late. Is there anything too hard for God?'"

What is amazing about this Word from the Lord is during prayer that morning while I was asking God about His promise to give me a husband, He told me to read Psalm 37:4 about delighting yourself in the Lord. He also had me read the entries in my journal and remember His promises to me and the things He had done previously in my life. So, the word the Pastor gave was confirmation concerning the prayer I prayed earlier that morning.

Then when my cousin and her husband came to visit us that next Saturday, I told them what the pastor said. That same night, while I was praying and reading, God took me through my journal again. I came across an entry that recounted a dream I once had about being late for a fashion show, which represented being out of place for a blessing because of a distraction that made me late. Just as I was about to ask God if it was too late for the blessing he had for me (because of distractions), He brought back to my remembrance what He had said through the pastor the week before, that "before I asked, He would answer," and the answer was, "It is not too late." Amazing, before I even asked the question, God had already answered me. Now this week He reminds me to delight myself in the Lord. So now I will study on how to delight myself in Him.

UPDATE

God blessed me with a wonderful husband in 2006, which proves there is nothing too hard for God.

Chapter 6

MY PURPOSE

The Sorrow of God's Heart

September 12, 2005

6.5

The Word of the Lord has come to you this day. The voice of the Lord has spoken. Take heed of the Word of the Lord. He has written your name in the Lamb's book of life and it shall not be removed. Trust in the Lord and do good and lean not to your own understanding. The Lord is good and greatly to be praised.

You have done a service to the Lord in that you have told how the Lord has blessed you. Because of this, the Lord has greatly multiplied your sorrow in that He has given you a burden for the people to intercede on their behalf to pray a covering over them to protect them and keep them, that the Lord will not destroy them, for they are a rebellious people.

They have ignored my warnings and my wrath is kindled against them. Dova, I choose not to destroy them, but you must pray for them to turn my wrath from them. It saddens my heart to see the things that people do to one another. I want them to live to enjoy the blessings of the Lord, to live with me forever in heaven but their heart is turned away from me.

They say they love me, but they treat each other with disdain. They don't understand the true meaning of "love thy neighbor as thyself." Most don't even understand what love is so they cannot even love their own selves. So, when they go to love their neighbor as themselves, their lack of love for themselves and their mistreatment of themselves causes them to mistreat their neighbor.

When women allow men to abuse them, how can they show someone else love when they do not respect themselves enough to demand love? When men destroy one another with drugs, alcohol, and immoral sexual activity, and then in turn allow themselves to be destroyed by the very same activity, how can they love their neighbor? How can men and women love their neighbor when they don't even love themselves enough to take care of themselves or their families?

My heart is grieved because of the mindset of the people. I want them to be transformed by the renewing of their minds so that this mind will be in them that was also in Christ Jesus. "If my people who are called by my name will humble themselves, and pray and seek my face, and turn from their wicked ways, then I will hear from heaven and will forgive their sin and heal their land." (2 Chronicles

7:14 NKJV)

I want them to know I love them, and I want to help them, but they must come to me with a humble heart. Too many people come to command a blessing. Standing on promises they do not understand. People say 'Lord you said this or that' but they have not done their part of the promise by humbling themselves, submitting themselves to me or even repenting of their sins, but expect me to keep my promise to bless them. They have their hand out to receive but they do not give with a pure heart, there is always a motive behind it. A pure heart gives because a person has a need without expecting to get it back. These people give with the express purpose of receiving again and are disappointed if they do not receive it back again with a hundred-fold return. Now it's no longer about helping one another, it's about what can I get out of it.

You must tell the people they have to change their ways; they must come to learn how to properly love themselves so they can properly love others. Only then will my wrath be completely turned away from them, until then they will see more devastation."

Chapter 6
A WORD FROM THE LORD
May 8, 2006
6.6

While I was in prayer this morning the Lord showed me that I will be transitioning from a rebellious teenager to an adult in the spirit realm. He said that when teenagers rebel it is usually because they are trying to establish their own identity, going from following Mom and Dad to leading their own lives. But because they do not know who they really are or how to find themselves, they tend to follow the lead of other people without knowing where following that person will lead them. They see popularity, boldness and confidence and want to pattern themselves after that person, but they really do not understand where that person's life will end up.

So it is with me spiritually. I have been following the lead of people who I felt were confident, strong, and popular. I have followed their lead not knowing where it would lead to. That is why I have been having dreams about being left behind. In each dream I'm following along with other people thinking I know where we are headed but once we get to a certain point it becomes clear that I don't know the directions to the destination or sometimes where the destination is. I always seem to get separated from the group somehow and because I don't know exactly where we are going or how to get there, I end up stranded somewhere, then I wake up.

God said I've tried to follow other people's ministries trying to prepare myself to be in ministry without knowing what the ministry is (walking in darkness without knowledge – *Chapter 9*). God has said it is time to stop following other people and follow the one He has chosen for me to follow, Jesus. When Elijah chose Elisha, it was because Elisha was who God told him to choose. Elijah did not make the decision himself. Elisha did not go after someone else; he went after the one that God chose for him to follow. When it was time for Elijah to leave, Elisha was ready to step up and take his place and carry on successfully. So it is with following Jesus: He is the one God chose for me to follow. Jesus trained the disciples and provided everything they would need (The Holy Ghost) so when he left, they were able to step up and take their place and carry on successfully. So must I step up and take my place and carry on successfully.

God also told me He was going to establish my fiance' on his job and settle him so that he has a foundation and from there He would bless him to be a blessing to others because of a heart and mind for the youth. God said starting from today for one year He is going to bless us financially and He is binding Satan's hand, and he will not be allowed to touch our finances because he was found as a thief and must restore seven-fold though it cost him the wealth of his house. (Proverbs 6:31 NKJV)

Within that year we must do all we can to eliminate our financial debt. Do not buy a lot of stuff, stay on track. Do not buy a new car. God will bless my car to last one more year, I must get it fixed, however. Do not buy Jimmy, Jr. a car yet let him get established with school first. Do not buy extra things for the house like fences or furniture. For one year just work on getting our finances in order. God gave me Psalm 112 as the scripture to stand on. After one year, God is going to allow Satan free access or rein in our finances but by then we will be in a much better position to handle whatever comes. We have a plan for paying off our debt. God says stick to that plan.

UPDATE

We were able to do the first part of what God said in that we did not buy cars or fix up the house or buy a lot of things, but the second part was much more difficult. We were not able to pay off all of our debt like we had hoped. As God said after that year Satan was given access to our finances and for the next seven years, we suffered some difficult financial hardships, medical bills, temporary layoffs, lowered wages, car accidents and more.

We got through it with God's help and learned so much in the process. With everything we went through it never came between us, it came against us but not between us, in fact we grew closer together. My husband is still on his job despite the many people who suffered from permanent layoffs there and despite all the temporary layoffs he had to go through. He is well established there now and has helped so many people in the process.

Chapter 6
WHAT THE LORD TOLD ME
June 17, 2006
6.7

This morning in prayer the Lord told me He has many blessing in store for Jimmy and I. Our wedding will go forth very smoothly, without a hitch. Our honeymoon will be a dream come true. He also said something is coming down the way that will be devastating to me, but Jimmy will be right there to help me through it, and it will strengthen my relationship with Jimmy and with God. He said I have to go through it but when I come out, I will be victorious and stronger and will be different person.

UPDATE

This word was brought to pass when we were married in the same month and the wedding and honeymoon were amazing. Then came the second part which was the death of my brother from cancer about eight months after the wedding. It was devastating but the devastating part had a second half that came after changing churches to attend church with my husband at his home church where he moved from.

The part that was devastating was learning things about myself that I did not know before and didn't like. I learned I had a lot of pride which was hard to accept considering I suffered from low self-esteem. God had taught me about pride then helped me understand how it affected my life. After coming to an understanding of what God was teaching me, He moved our church membership back to the town where we live.

I definitely grew from the experience and am much stronger that before, the experience also made me a different person. I have a better understanding of who I am and the person God made me to be. God definitely fulfilled His Word.

REFLECTION

A LITTLE PAUSE FOR THE CAUSE

The next chapter might look as if my life has taken a step backward but when you look at the date at the top, you will notice that it is starting in the year 1998 and then it goes forward from there. This brings up an interesting point however, that sometimes you will go through thing over and over again. Sometime when you think you have gotten ahead you find you have taken a few steps back. The good news is God has given us weapons to use to overcome the enemy. Sometimes you go backward because you are being tested on what you have learned, and you need to bring back to remembrance the things God has taught you so you can **Stand** on His **Word**. Do not let yourself get discouraged when this happens just trust God to bring you through.

Chapter 7

Introduction 7.1

THE PROMISES OF GOD

My Testimony

STANDING ON THE PROMISES OF GOD

Twenty years ago, in 1985 the Lord filled me with the Holy Ghost. It was the most exciting event of my life. God began to show me things I did not know were possible for someone my age, miracle and abilities and authority over the enemy. I was so excited and so on fire for God.

About a year later I got married, which was my first mistake. As time moved on, I was really growing in the Word and learning so much and that is when the second mistake happened. After learning about our authority over the devil I made the mistake of challenging him and got royally whooped, so badly that I ended up leaving the church, got a divorce and was a back slider for many years. However, God in His infinite mercy pursued me and brought me to state of surrender in 1995, ten years after getting filled with the Holy Ghost.

I remember sitting in the middle of my bed pleading with God to restore my relationship with Him, I heard Him clearly say to me, "read Isaiah 54." Most of my Bible study at that time had been either in the New Testament or a variety of different verse through a series study so I was not even aware that Isaiah had a chapter 54 in it. When I read the first sentence I was blown away because it reads "Sing O barren, thou that didst not bare." That was me; barren and had been told by doctors that I could not have children.

As I read on, it was amazing how this chapter matched so much of what I was going through in my life at that time. When I finished reading it, I told God, "you put this in here just for me, you knew I'd read it years later." At that point I felt God was saying to me, "I know you. I see and know who you are." Throughout this chapter God made me several promises. A promise to remove the shame of my youth, a promise of peace, a promise of protection and a promise of a future. Since then, He divided them into these promises:

- A promise of Protection – Psalm 91
- A promise of Peace – Isaiah 54
- A promise of Blessing – Deuteronomy 28: 1-14
- A promise of a Future – Proverbs 31: 10-31

I have been standing on these promises and He has kept them.
- I walk in the promise of Protection each night when God protects my home from intrusion and keeps me safe on the streets as I drive from place to place.

- I walk in the promise of Peace because I have peace with God. Also, when my mother passed away His spirit of peace enveloped me and carried me for months.
- I see the promise of Blessing each time I look at my house, my car, my job and know there is no way I should have them, (but God). I did not have the money or the credit for them, but God made a way.
- I walk in the promise of a Future when I look back over my life and recognize that the things I used to do, I don't want to do anymore, the places I use to go, I don't want to go anymore and the things I used to settle for, I don't settle for anymore. God removed the shame of my youth and clothed me in the beauty of holiness. He has changed my life so much and I am no longer the person I use to be.

I thank God for Salvation through Christ Jesus, and the Gift of the Holy Ghost.

Chapter 7
GREAT AND PRECIOUS PROMISES
September 2, 1998
7.2

God has given us great and precious promises wrapped up as gifts and stored in treasure boxes locked with keys and He's given us all the keys. It is up to us to use the keys to unlock the treasure to all the gifts of promise.

Example: Deuteronomy 28: 3-14 says, "Blessed shall you be in the city and blessed shall you be in the field. Blessed shall be the fruit of your body and the fruit of your ground and the fruit of your cattle, the increase of your kine. Blessed shall be your baskets and your store. Blessed shall you be when come in and when you go out."

"He will cause your enemies to be defeated before your face. He will command a blessing in your storehouses and all that you set your hand unto. He will open to you His good treasure the heavens to give rain to your land in its season and bless all the work of your hands. You shall lend and not borrow. You shall be the head and not the tail. You shall be above only and not beneath."

These are just some of the promises He has given us as gifts. He has already given them to us; they are in our possession already. All we have to do is use the keys to unlock the treasure. The keys to these promised blessings are found in verses 1, 2, 13b and 14; if you diligently obey the voice of the Lord your God which you are commanded this day and are careful to observe them and not turn aside from any of the words which I command you this day, to the left or to the right, to go after other gods to serve them.

These keys will unlock all the treasure of promise from God for you to enjoy. However, you first need to have the Master Key that comes when you accept salvation through Jesus Christ, who paid the penalty of our sins, and you are filled with the Holy Ghost, these two things will give you the power to be obedient to God. Remember He has already given you the gifts so there is no need to keep asking for it. When someone gives you something and you decide to receive it, you wouldn't go back to that person and ask them for it again because you already have it but you can't enjoy the benefits of it if you don't unwrap it or use the key to unlock the treasure.

This is not to say that your gift cannot be hindered, we do have an enemy, however it is up to us to claim our gifts of promise and bind the thief. Matthew 16:19 says, "And I will give you the keys of the kingdom of heaven and whatsoever you bind on earth shall be bound in heaven and whatsoever you loose on earth shall be loosed in heaven. So, bind the enemy (thief) and loose your promises. For God has already given you the keys.

Chapter 7
THE PROMISE OF GOD
January 24, 2000
7.3

In the day of my Holy visitation from God,

I was told to write down these words.

The Lord thy God is with thee. He will not leave thee nor forsake thee. He will love thee until the end of the world and beyond through all eternity. Speak those things which be not as though they were and never cease to believe. For in the day you cease to believe them, they will become no more.

Thou art a holy child chosen from birth to do a mighty work for the Lord, and that work which you will do is divinely inspired by God. You will walk according to the laws of the Word and not according to your own ability or goodness. Know this that the Lord is God, and He picks whom He chooses.

All the things you have asked for down through the years you are about to receive because you have believed God and been found faithful.

- Salvation for my family members

- A saved man of God for a mate
- A three-bedroom home of my own
- My own business in design
- To be a better aunt
- To be more diligent about the things I do
- To be a soul winner for God
- To have a great ministry for Christ
- A newer car
- Children

Isaiah 54, Proverbs 31: 10-31, Deuteronomy 28: 1-14

Although I cannot do these things in and of myself, "I can do all things through Christ who strengthens me" (Philippians 4:13 NKJV), and the Lord will bless the work of your hands and "all you set your hand unto." (Deuteronomy 28:8 paraphrased) The Lord tells us, you shall be free to do all things by design that you desire. Never give up and never be discouraged for I will be with you. I have anointed your hands for healing, for miracles and for design.

What I have chosen for you is not for anyone else and what I have chosen for others is not for you. Walk in what I have given you. There are generations of blessings that have been bestowed upon you. You will see things no one else can see. You will see angels ascending and descending from heaven. You will see them do work upon the earth that others cannot see.

You are a gifted child and people will not understand you, but others will flock to you to receive what God has given you and you will tell them of the goodness of God. You have been blessed with the gift of angels, to know their purpose upon the earth. You are to work with them to the glory of God. People will call you strange and others will come to you, not even knowing why, to ask you for prayer. As you pray for them, you will dispatch angels to go with them for protection, healing, and directions.

Chapter 7

THE FOUR PROMISES OF GOD

July 2, 2002

7.4

Today God revealed something awesome to me. After watching a prominent bishop on one of the Christian broadcast channels and hearing confirmation of many things God has said to me, God showed me:

<u>Who I am;</u>

<u>Who He has made me to be;</u>

<u>How He has blessed me;</u> and

<u>How He will protect me.</u>

- *Who I am:* Isaiah 54 — The barren one.
- *Who He has made me:* Proverbs 31: 10-31 — A Virtuous Woman.
- *How He has blessed me:* Deuteronomy 28: 1-14 — I am blessed coming in and blessed going out. He has blessed the work of my hands and all that I set my hands unto.
- *How He has protected me:* Psalm 91 — I dwell in the secret place of the Most High. He is my refuge and

my fortress. *Isaiah 54:17* says, "No weapon formed against me shall prosper."

I am excited about how God sees me and about who I am in Him. I look forward to being all of who He created me to be.

Chapter 7
ISAIAH 54
2002
7.5

Isaiah 54 represents the blessing that is tied to me buying my new house. It will give me more space for my sewing and creativity, more space for hospitality so I can take in guests if I need to or have room if I adopt children.

It also talks about my Maker being my husband, meaning He will take care of me, provide for me, and protect me. He had hidden His face from me for a little while because I had married without His permission and He was displeased with that, but with great mercies He has gathered me (brought me back).

I also opened my mouth and challenged the devil openly and took a bad whooping because of it (which I mentioned in a previous chapter). God promised I would not be haunted by the shame of my youth. It is behind me. He has given me a covenant of peace.

He has promised that even though my enemies might gather together against me, they shall not prevail because no weapon formed against me shall prosper. As I move out and move up, it allows someone else to move out and move up, too.

Chapter 7
FOUR GREAT AND PRECIOUS PROMISES
March 8, 2004

7.6

I need to change the way I think. Too many times I allow Satan to trick me by getting my thinking out of whack. I begin to believe the lies he tells me, such as nobody cares about me or likes me. I will never succeed at my dream career. I will never have the joy of motherhood. I am not smart enough to start and maintain my own business. I will never have a successful ministry in the church.

God gave me four great and precious promises:
- A promise of blessing – Deuteronomy 28:1-14
- A promise of protection – Psalm 91
- A promise to shape me into a Virtuous Woman – Proverbs 31:10-31
- A promise to remove the shame of my past – Isaiah 54

He also said He knows the plans He has for me. Plans to prosper me and not to harm me. Plans to give me a hope and a future. (Jeremiah 29:11) I need to keep my mind stayed on Jesus so I can overcome the thoughts the enemy tries to bring across my mind. I need to remember what the Bible says: meditate on the Word, believe the Word, and have faith in the Word.

I also need to resist the temptation of the enemy to gossip, be lazy, have a negative attitude, be self-righteous and talk too much. (Lord help me to remember that I have two ears to hear and one mouth to speak, which means I should listen twice as much as I speak.)

Satan also tries to use sleep to try to cause me to miss what God was trying to say to me. I must remember that "Whatsoever I bind on earth shall be bound in heaven and whatsoever I loose on earth shall be loosed in heaven." (Matthew 18:18 paraphrased) Also "No weapon that is formed against me shall prosper." (Isaiah 54:17 paraphrased)

REFLECTION

HISTORY (His Story)

All throughout Biblical history we learn many things: Things about the creation of the world, the fall of man, the destruction of everything on earth due to flood, the choice of the Israelites as God's people, their captivity and rescue from the Egyptians, all their wanderings and lack of faithfulness to God. But in all the teaching and preaching we hear about the *history* of the Children of Israel sometimes we overlook ***"His Story,"*** God's Story, the story He is telling us about Himself, about His patience with us, His love for us, His power and ability to keep and sustain us and to provide for us. Even when we do see these things while reading the stories, sometimes we forget that the purpose of the story is not only to tell the history, but it is God's way of showing us who He is.

Let's look at a few examples. When we look at the creation of the world, the Bible tells us that God created the heavens and the earth and all the birds of the air and the fish of the sea and all the animals of the earth, the plants, grasses and trees. Now this goes from Genesis 1:1-25, but in verse 26 He says, "Let us make man in our image after our likeness and let him have dominion over…." Now right here we normally look at this as being the story of the creation of man but if we really look at it, God is telling us His Story.

"Let us," first tells us that God is not alone. He is talking to someone not Himself.

Second that He wants man to bear His image and likeness. What is God's image and likeness? Well, let's go up in history a bit to the time of Jesus. When Jesus was conceived, it was of the Holy Ghost, making Him the only begotten (sired) of the Father. (John 1:14) In Luke 3:21-22, it tells us about the baptism of Christ by John the Baptist and how the Holy Ghost descended like a dove upon Him and a voice from heaven said, "Thou art my beloved son; in thee I am well pleased." This tells us who the "us" was in Genesis 1:26. "Us" is the Father, Son, and Holy Ghost. They are a family. Therefore, He made man in His likeness, male and female created He them and He told them to multiply, and they became a family.

Also, in God's likeness man is a three-part being; body, soul, and spirit. God is also body, soul, and spirit. Jesus is the bodily form of God; the Father is the soul of God (mind, will and emotions); and of course, the Holy Ghost is the spirit of God. One God, three function. Because of this likeness, dominion was given unto us over all the earth.

We are also made in God's image. An image is the

reproduction of the form of a person. One that closely resembles another. An optically formed counterpart of an object especially one formed by a lens or mirror. A representation, to mirror or reflect. When you look in a mirror, the image you see should look exactly like you and everything you do it does. If you raise your hand, it raises its hand. If you scratch your head, it scratches its head and so on. However, it cannot do anything independent from you, it does not have the ability. It can only do what you do. This was the intent of God when creating man. We were to be the mirror image of God in the earth, able to do exactly what He does, but sin marred that image, and we lost a lot of that ability until Christ came.

Although we are not God nor are we gods, we are the reflected image of God; we have His ability to reason and to make or create things. We have the ability to speak and to "call those things which be not as though they were." (Romans 4:17b) In other words, calling things into existence as God did with creation, like calling the dead back to life, deliverance to the oppressed, calling healing to those who are sick. By giving us the gift of the Holy Ghost, God has given us the ability to do the very same things Christ did here on the earth and even greater things, as he said.

Through the gift of the Holy Ghost and the abilities we have been given, it shows us more about who God is, what He is about, and again we see His love for us. We see His compassion and through the birth, death, and resurrection of Jesus, we see God's great ability to forgive. He created us, gave us life, and gives us all the things we need to sustain that life. He still gives us free will, the option to choose or reject Him. Through this we see His patience, temperance (self-control), and His faith in us.

Another way that God is telling us His Story is the fact that God desires to have a relationship with us, a close personal relationship with us. In Genesis 3:8-11, we read a conversation between God and Adam.

Adam hears God's voice as he was walking in the garden in the cool of the day, and Adam and Eve hid themselves and God asks, "where art thou?" and they respond. What we see here is a conversation between Adam, Eve, and God. A physical conversation one on one, which also shows God was physically present with them.

Sometimes we have this image of God being somewhere out in the heavens far away from us. But God wants us to know He is right here present with us. Matthew 28:20b says, "and lo I am with you always, even unto the end of the world." Another scripture says "I will never leave you nor forsake you." (Hebrews 13:5b)

What does all this mean? It means that God wants to have a close personal relationship with us, to walk with us in the cool of the day, to have conversations with us, not just us spewing out request all the time. God wants us to listen and hear what He has to say. Sometimes He wants us to just sit quiet in His presence and sometimes He just wants us to listen. Through God's word, we also see that God is personally interested in every aspect of our life, even the details, the things that are important to us. 1 Peter 5:7 says, "casting all your care upon Him; for He careth for you." (KJV)

There are many people who do not have a relationship with their parents for one reason or another. It might be due to being adopted into another family or they might have grown up in foster care, one or the other parent might not have been in the home as they grew up, or they just might not get along with their parents or many other reasons. But for one reason or another the relationship is broken. Then there are those who have a slightly distant relationship. They speak and they get along every now and then, but you would not say they have a close relationship. Then there are those who do have a close relationship with their parents. They talk all the time, they enjoy each other's company, visiting as often as possible, and they look after each other. Now out of all the previous descriptions, which relationship do you think God wants to have with us?

Think about the relationship God had with Moses, He talked with Moses and Moses talked with Him. God not only showed Moses His power, but He also allowed him to be an instrument of that power when he faced Pharaoh and delivered the children of Israel out of Egyptian bondage, and led them through the wilderness and up to the door of the promised land. He allowed Moses the privilege of seeing part of His glory while they spent time together talking, and because of that the glory of God was all over Moses insomuch that people could not look on the face of Moses because of the glow. This is the kind of relationship God wants with us. We should be so close to God that instead of seeing us they see the glow of God's glory on us and we become instruments of God's power against the enemy for the deliverance of others by leading them to Christ.

We can also look at God's relationship with Jesus. Because they are Father and Son, they are quite close. Jesus introduced us to God as Father, which is a more intimate relationship than the Jews had with God before Christ came. Jesus always did what His Father told him to do, and Jesus stayed in close contact with His Father. Jesus was even obedient unto death allowing Him to be the instrument that God our Father used for our deliverance out of bondage to sin, which allows Jesus to lead those who will follow Him through the wilderness of this world and into the promised land of heaven.

The deliverance of the Children of Israel from Egypt shows God's ability to deliver. The book of Revelations shows God's unending love when He revealed His plan for our future after our death. When Christ Jesus came, He showed us what the express image of His person looks like. He showed exactly how God intended for us to live. We see Christ Jesus defying the laws of nature when He walked on water. He was not limited by this earthly realm (for example, the transfiguration). He showed us how to operate in the same manner, with the same authority He has. He healed the sick, raised the dead, delivered those in bondage, and opened blinded eyes and much, much more. Everything he did we can do.

Another way God tells us His Story is through the work of the Holy Spirit. God has called us and ordained us to participate in His work in the earth by what the Holy Ghost does through us. I remember when a previous co-worker of mine was suffering from severe back pain, it was so bad that he was scheduled to have surgery to correct it. The Holy Ghost prompted me to ask him if I could pray for him and he agreed. A few hours later, I saw him at break time and asked him how he was feeling, and he said the pain was completely gone. I saw him a few days later and he said he was still pain free and that he had canceled the surgery.

After he left the company, I ran into a close friend of his who said he was still pain free and talking about what God had done for him. It was quite exciting to be part of a miracle of God and to watch Him work so quickly and completely. So, when we go to God in prayer lets seek Him to find out what part of His Story He wants to tell through us.

Chapter 8

Introduction 8.1

I AM WHO GOD SAYS I AM

There is an excitement that goes along with finding out who I am, the real me. The "me" behind the mask that I wore for so long. There are definitions in this chapter that explain how God said He sees me. When I look back, I can see it. Thank God some things have changed for the better and some things are now as they should be. Let God show you who you really are. Do not be afraid to remove the masks you have been wearing. You look better without them.

Chapter 8
LEARNING TO HIT THE TARGET
December 26, 2002

8.2

During my time in prayer this morning, the Father in heaven showed me a part of myself. He showed me how effective or ineffective my words can be. That reminded me of a conversation with my niece yesterday about all the things I wanted to say to her which reminded me of something my brother said to me once. He said that I always like trying to fix things or try to make them work out. I realized this is true. My hope is to tell people things they should know, like in my conversation with my niece, to try to help her correct a problem. My goal is to get people together and get them to talk so they can repair broken relationships or so they can forgive one another.

While thinking about this, I asked God, "Why am I like this?" and He said immediately, "Because I made you that way." God said I'm a fixer and a fixer is someone who likes to make things right. He said my words are for a purpose, but they are being misdirected. God gave me the analogy of an arrow being aimed at a target, but my arrows are missing the mark. He said my words are arrows and although they might be true and right, if God has not prepared that person to receive them, my words are like arrows that miss the target. He said people are like moving targets and it can be hard to hit a moving target.

God said that I am an archer, and my words are my arrows, but just like a new archery student, not only is the bullseye missed but also the intended target altogether. God wants to teach me how to become a proficient archer. Sometimes I will hit the intended target but because of not waiting for God to position them to hear what He gave me to say to them, the arrow missed the bullseye and I ended up wounding them instead.

God said by waiting for Him, not only will He position the target, but He will also guide the arrows, so that they hit the bullseye every time. God wants me to use the words He has given me, but He wants me to wait on Him to choose the right time and place.

Chapter 8
I AM WHO GOD SAYS I AM
8.3

In an effort to transform the way I see myself; God gave me a word study to help me see myself differently and better understand the way He sees me.

PRECIOUS – I am precious in the eyesight of GOD, Isaiah 43:4 – of high cost or worth; valuable; dear; beloved; <u>Affectedly</u> <u>dainty</u> or over-refined.

- Affected = assumed or simulated to impress others.
- Impress = to produce a vivid often favorable effect on, to establish firmly in the mind.
- Dainty = <u>delicate</u>ly beautiful – of refined taste.
- Delicate= <u>exquisite</u>ly or pleasingly fine, easily damaged.
- Exquisite= <u>beautiful</u>ly made or designed.
- Beautiful = a quality that pleases the senses or mind.
- Refined = free from coarseness or vulgarity, free from impurity, <u>precise</u> to a fine degree, exact.
- Precise = strictly distinguished from others, definite

WONDERFUL — "I am fearfully and wonderfully made." Psalm 139:14 — Capable of <u>exciting</u> <u>wonder</u>, <u>astonishing</u> or <u>marvelous</u>.

- Excite = to stir to activity, stimulate, provoke to raise to a higher energy level.
- Wonder = one that arouses awe, surprise or admiration, marvel.
- Astonishing = to fill with sudden wonder or amazement.
- Marvelous = of the highest kind of quality, splendid, <u>admirable, excellent</u>.
- Admirable = deserving <u>admiration.</u>
- Admiration — admire = to regard with wonder, approval, to esteem, respect.
- Excellent = of the highest or finest quality, exceptionally good, superb.

JEWEL — I am a jewel in His crown. Malachi 3:18 — A precious stone, Gem; An ornament of precious metal set with gems.

UNIQUE — There is no one else like me — Being the only one of its kind. Being without an equal or equivalent.

AMAZING — To fill with surprise or wonder, astonish.

CREATIVE – Characterized by originality, imaginative.

JOYFUL – A source of pleasure.

FUNNY – Causing laughter and amusement.

PLEASANT – Pleasing, agreeable delightful, <u>pleasing</u> or favorable in manner, <u>amiable</u>.
- Pleasing = to make glad, give enjoyment or satisfaction to
- Amiable = good-natured, friendly

AWESOME – Inspiring or characterized by <u>awe</u>.
- Awe = an emotion mingled with reverence, dread and wonder; respect tinged with fear.

TEACHABLE – Able to be instructed.

WITTY – Having or showing wit, cleverly humorous, the ability to perceive and express humorously the relationship or similarity between seemingly <u>incongruous</u> or <u>disparate</u> things.
- Incongruous = not consistent with what is logical, customary or expected, inappropriate
- Disparate = completely distinct or different,

dissimilar.

PERSONABLE – Pleasing in appearance or personality.

INTELLIGENT – The capability to acquire and apply knowledge. The facility of thought or reason, superior powers of mind.

MAJESTIC – Supreme authority or power (given by Christ through the Holy Ghost); regal dignity, splendor, and grandeur.

FIERCE – <u>Intense</u> or ardent: for example – fierce loyalty.
- Intense = extreme in degree, strength, or size, involving or showing great concentration strain, deeply felt, profound.

RAMBUNCTIOUS – <u>Boisterous</u>, unruly.
- Boisterous = rough and stormy, noisy, high spirited, unrestrained.

TRUTHFUL – Consistently telling the truth, Honest, <u>Corresponding</u> to reality.
- Corresponding = to be in agreement, harmony, or conformity, to be similar or equal to.

WISE — Every wise woman builds her house Proverbs 14:1a — Having wisdom, judicious.

- Wisdom = understanding of what is true, right, or lasting.
- Judicious = having or exhibiting sound judgment, having or showing common sense, prudent.
- Common Sense = inborn good judgment.
- Prudent = wise in handling practical matters, careful regarding one's own interests, provident, careful about one's conduct, circumspect.
- Provident= providing for future needs or events, frugal, economical, having knowledge or awareness, knowing, discerning.

MOTIVATED — To stir to action, provide with a motive.

- Motive = an impulse that causes one to act in a particular manner.

These words all describe the person God says I am. Understanding who I am helps me understand why I do the things that I do, allows me to make the changes that need to be made and helps prevent Satan from using my weaknesses against me that would normally cause me to give in to temptation. Who does God say you are? What words does God say describe you?

Chapter 8

GOD'S PLAN FOR MY LIFE

April 27, 2005

8.4

As I was praying this morning, God began showing me His plan for my life. A few days ago, He showed me through a message I heard on TV that He is in complete control and that sin was in the plan of God from the beginning. Not because it was His will for it to be so, but because He knew it would happen. He knew what people would do.

We as people are put here on the earth to show forth the glory of God in the earth. I was therefore placed in the earth at this time in history because God knew I would show forth His glory in the earth, not because I'm so great but because He planned it that way, to use me as a vessel for His use.

Then Jesus asked me where I see myself in the next five years. My response was "I see myself married, hopefully. I see myself as a better teacher, more successful in my interior decorating business, more knowledgeable in the Word." Then He asked me if I would like to know where He sees me in five years. Of course, my answer was "yes." This was His response: "I'd like to see a thousand people saved through you and millions of people won for Christ through your life. I'd like to see miracles performed through you, lives transformed, and many people affected by you for Christ." I was stunned. Here I was thinking in the natural and Jesus was talking spiritual. His plan is better. It makes me focus more on being a vessel for His use. While continuing in prayer, God had me read Deuteronomy 6:18 and Ephesians 5:26 and then told me that He was going to make me a woman of power and authority without limitations.

It's evening now and while still in prayer, God made me realize that I'm shy. For a while now Jesus has been trying to get me to see myself as I really am, a very shy person. This realization came while talking to God about not knowing how to talk to men. It's hard to know what to say sometimes and that would cause me to freeze up.

This brought back to my mind something someone once said to me, which was, "I didn't realize you were shy." It took me by surprise because I never thought of myself as shy. God, however, helped me realize that this is the real me and because of being shy it has caused me to act like other people that seemed to be more confident than myself, people whom I admired. Unfortunately, it also caused me to pick up some habits that were not so good, habits that were a result of some abusive people in my past, like snapping back at people, gossiping, and bragging to make myself look better. The Lord made me realize that I have been imitating others for so long that it caused me to forget who I was. By acknowledging this truth about myself, God said He can use me better as that shy girl because then my confidence is in Him and not in myself or the imitation of others I have been hiding behind.

Chapter 8
REALIZING WHO I AM
May 2, 2005
8.5

The Lord tells me to be myself but who am I? All this year He has been showing me things about myself. Uncovering layers of things. Yesterday we talked about the real me. The real me likes to sleep late and go to bed late because of my earlier work habits. I used to work the afternoon shift in Retail and when you are in management you are required to be there until the store closes and everything is put away, so it always caused me to be up late at night which resulted in waking up later the next day. I did this for about fourteen years.

After changing to a daytime position, a friend and I were talking and the subject of prayer came up and she commented that she gets up early for prayer (5:30 a.m.), every morning. I remember thinking "maybe I should do that," which caused me to start getting up early ever day around 6 a.m. but that is not the real me.

The real me is not athletic but I have always daydreamed about being a very active person, one who eats right, exercises, has a lot of friends and is very popular. The real me would rather watch TV than read; however, in recent years, I have read a lot of books that I thought would help me change and become a new person, but they didn't.

The reason these things are important is it helps me identify problem areas in my life. For example: After hearing my friend say that she got up early for prayer, it made me want to do the same thing because I thought it would make me more pleasing to God. Another thought was being more athletic (jogging, aerobics and lifting weights), would help me improve my looks and make me more attractive to men, or that reading books to help me becoming a better person would make me more acceptable to women and help me turn them into friends and thus be more popular.

God made me realize that none of that has worked and it is a slap in His face because it all means that I'm not happy with the way He made me and He should have made me like this person or that person, so I decided that I'm going to fix it. There is nothing wrong with getting up early for prayer or exercising or reading. There is a problem when my motives are wrong. The decision to do these things should be because I want to be more like Christ. Not to be like someone else or to attract people to me or to impress people so they will like me. It is important for me to learn to love myself for who I am, the person God created me to be. While learning to love myself, others will learn to love me for me.

All my life people have made me feel inferior as though something was wrong with me or I wasn't normal, but there is nothing wrong with me; I am just fine the way God made me, tall, slim and beautiful, and He has gifted me in art and design.

Making the decision to get up early for prayer or not doesn't matter as long as I'm faithful to spend time in prayer, God said choose a time and be faithful to that time. Whether it is 6:00 a.m. or 9:00 a.m. Don't get up 5 or 10 minutes later but be consistent with the time I set. God is not upset about getting up at 5:30 a.m. or 6:00 am.; what bothers Him is that I don't keep my commitment to the time I set. Even if it is 6:20 a.m. or 9:15 a.m. every morning, be faithful to that time.

Deciding to exercise every day or once a week, should be for health purposes not to build my body to attract men. Exercise is good, but my reasons should be to help keep my limbs and joints from getting stiff, to keep my circulation going and for my overall health. Instead of trying to impress other people, I want to strive to please God.

He took the time to show me these things and how they are putting me in bondage. He has set me free. Little by little, He is peeling off the layers of junk to reveal the real person inside. Wanting to be an extraordinary person, means waiting for God to finish His work in me. Instead of continuing to try to be like other people, who in God's eyes might be ordinary (the world), He wants me to be the centerpiece He designed me to be (a saint). Like in the fashion show, I keep trying to be a regular model on the runway, when God is trying to prepare me to be the main showstopper, the bride for His audience of One.

REFLECTION

Chapter 9
Introduction 9.1
THE DREAM

Dreams can be powerful. Have you ever had dreams come true? I have, many times, and now believe that this is what we call "déjà vu," where people think they have done something before, when in reality, they are dreams that we have that have come true. What makes me believe that is several times having a dream and waking up remembering the dream and the details of the dream and then days or months later experiencing the events that happened in the dream and right away I remember dreaming it before it happened.

Then there are some dreams that relay a message. I have had some of these dreams multiple times. It is the same dream, but the details are a little different. That is what this chapter is about because a few of the dreams have been repeated over the years. After finally going to God and asking Him about them, He revealed the meaning behind them to me and the next few pages reveal what I learned.

Chapter 9
THE DREAM
May 5, 2003
9.2

About a month ago or more, I woke up from a dream, a recurring dream about being late for a fashion show that I am supposed to be in. It's put on by a friend of mine who is a designer. In each dream, I'm always late due to being off somewhere trying to help someone or distracted by someone or something, which causes me to always get there just as the show is beginning, but I'm not dressed or ready and the show goes on without me.

In this last dream, I came in and started getting myself ready, trying to get dressed, putting on accessories, and getting my hair together. While getting dressed, two women who were in the show came backstage, and I asked them to help me dress for the show. The outfit was one of my own because the rack that should have had the clothes on it for me was not there. My sweater choice was purple with gold beading all over it with a black skirt. While looking for a hat to match, I kept asking the women for help, but they just laughed and mocked me and would not help. Finally, as the last person walked up to the runway, it made me realize that the show was over, and it was too late. As the designer came backstage, I began to apologize for missing the show. She said that it was all right as she tried to catch her breath because she was full of exhilaration from the success of the show.

I woke up realizing that once again it was the same dream, and it really upset me. I began to seek the Lord about it to understand why this same dream kept coming to me and here is what the Lord did: In a vision He took me back to the fashion show, the dressing room. He had me recall the events of the dream, the distractions in the beginning, and preparing myself for the show. He asked me to recall my color choices, which were purple and black with a black hat and black shoes. He showed me that black represents being without light, or being in darkness, that wearing a hat and shoes in black represents walking in darkness without knowledge or wisdom. Purple is the color of royalty, so my choice was to dress myself in royalty without knowledge or wisdom, to walk in darkness (not having an understanding of where you're going or the direction you're headed in). This was my choice in an effort try to fit into the show. Then He showed me that being late was due to allowing myself to be distracted by other people and things. Also, I was not invited to be in this show, but was trying to put myself in it. (In previous dreams I was invited to be in the show but still never arrived in time.)

Now you might ask, "what does all this mean?" The dream represents my spiritual life (purpose) where God has asked me to participate in His plan that He has prepared (the show) but instead distractions come by people and things around me so that when the trial comes, I am not prepared (because without a purpose, it's hard to know my place) and ready to perform (step up on the runway) as God has planned. (When you do not know where you fit in, you try to fit in anywhere you can). After arriving late, I started rushing to prepare myself and put on the things that I thought would work (dressing myself). In this instance, trying to put myself in someone else's show (God's plan for someone else).

He made me realize that my focus was on other people's ministries and trying to be like them instead of focusing on the ministry God has for me. While watching them, my efforts turned into attempts to find ways be included in the type of ministry (show) they were in. God reminded me that you cannot go to other designers' shows and dress yourself and try to include yourself in their show. The designers themselves choose what you will wear and assign someone to help dress you, or you will be out of place and will not fit in with the theme of the show. When the designer dresses you, you become an important part of the show and each person has his or her place. God said He is the designer of my life (for His purpose) and He wants to dress me for His show. The preparation is life and the one who assists in dressing you is the Holy Ghost and the show is my presentation before Him.

Then God showed me His plan for my part in His show. He showed me the dress He has prepared for me and it is beautiful. It is a white wedding dress. A dress that is whiter than white, insomuch that it glows. It is covered with pearls, lace, diamonds and it is full of flounces. The headpiece is amazing. It has feathers, diamond, pearls and much more. God said, "This is what I want you to wear," and He showed me the contrast between my choice of what to wear and what He had chosen for me.

The significance of this is that during a fashion show there are many designs presented in various colors and styles but the bride is always the highlight of the show. Everyone else steps aside as the bride takes over the runway and completes the show. God has shown me that I had prepared myself to be just a regular model in the show when He was preparing me to be the bride of the show. He said, "Let me dress you in the beauty of holiness and prepare you to be the bride I created you to be," the Bride of Christ. With that He led me on the runway to present me before the Father, an audience of one.

Chapter 9

REVELATION OF THE DREAM
February 2, 2005
9.3

SPIRITUAL MEANING OF BEING LEFT BEHIND

While spending time in prayer this morning God showed me that He is about to take me higher in Him. He made me realize that Satan has been holding me back, hindering me in my prayers, that the first part of my day should be a tithe to God spent in prayer and bible study. I have robbed God in my prayer time by not using the time frame He gave me correctly. Satan knows that I am a powerful weapon in prayer, and he is trying to keep God from using me against him. How has he hindered me? Keeping me busy, interfering with my sleep time, and using TV.

So as of today, God has put me on a TV fast. No television for one month. God has said I am behind in my spiritual life, and I have a lot to catch up on. So, He put me on an accelerated course. He said it will be hard and may cause me to cry sometimes but it will be worth it even though the realization that it should have been done sooner will be a little frustrating.

God said the dreams about being left behind are because my spiritual growth is being stunted. In one dream I was carrying luggage, books, and bags, and they were slowing me down. Other people that were with me were not helping me, nor did they carry any bags of their own. After waking up and thinking about the dream, it made me wondered why I was the only one carrying bags. The Lord revealed to me that it was old baggage in my life that needed to be gotten rid of because it is slowing me down.

While still wondering why these same dreams keep plaquing me, God helped me realize what He is trying to show me. In these dreams I am going somewhere, there are always people with me and things are going all right but when we get close to the destination, we get separated, I'd fall behind, or get distracted and leave.

God is letting me see my spiritual life. When I am close to my destination, I've been distracted, separated; I've fallen behind and, in some areas, left behind. This is the reason for the TV fast and the accelerated growth training. God said there is so much more to learn about Him and that He is about to expose me to many new things. He compared it this way:

- He caused me to remember when I worked for a company in California, and was the assistant manager. I worked with several college students and did not see the manager much because of our schedule, so most of my time was spent working with the students. One day it dawned on me that this was a problem because there was no adult stimulation. This realization became clear one day after talking to a woman during a training meeting who was telling me some things about her life, career, and family, and halfway through our conversation I realized I didn't understand what she was talking about and hadn't even heard of some of the things she was mentioning. That is what caused me to recognize that my social growth had been stunted. Being around college students kept me in that mindset while I was being left behind by my peers in the more important things in life. There were no challenges to stimulate me or make me want to grow up.

- I was content until God showed me through that experience that there was more to life. That led me to leave that job and go to work for another company where the people were more mature. It was more challenging and created the desire to be more like people my age, but many times I felt out of place. Even though that was many years ago, God is saying that it's still the same today in 2005, participating in immature things, being focused on things that are not important are causing my spiritual growth to be stunted.

This is the reason for the dreams. God said He is going to bring me out and put me around people who will challenge me and help me mature, one of which will be my husband (at this time, God hadn't revealed who he had in mind for me to marry). God said I have been content with my spiritual status, and it has kept me from growing due to fear of being further rejected. I tend to strive to achieve things to attain a level of acceptance and try to relate to people but for whatever reason they still reject me. My thinking was, if they saw all the things I know how to do, maybe they would accept me, but the opposite was true. The more I did the more they rejected me. This, too, has caused a stunt in my spiritual growth because now instead of wanting to grow, fear of rejection has caused me to stagnate. So, the accelerated growth project will help me to mature spiritually so I will not be left behind.

Chapter 9
THE REVELATION OF A DREAM II
April 6, 2005
9.4

THE SPIRITUAL MEANING OF BEING LEFT BEHIND AGAIN

I had another dream about being separated from a group of people and being left behind, and they go on to wherever they are going without me. This caused me to wake up angry. In this dream, I was out of town for a training meeting for my job. My boss was driving the van and several employees were in it. While coming out of the hotel and walking toward the van, the driver started driving off without me. I tried to get their attention by waiving my hands and running after them, but they kept going. A couple of guys saw me and offered to give me a ride to catch up with them. After getting in the car, we followed the van, but it made a couple of turns that we could not keep up with. Then they asked me where the van was going to, and they would just take me there. The problem was I didn't know where the meeting was being held. So, I couldn't tell them where to go. Then I woke up.

I immediately sought God to help me understand this dream. He helped me realize that in most of my dreams like this, I am going somewhere with a group of people but the location of the intended destination is not clear. This causes me to be unable keep going on when left behind because of not knowing where to go. Also, He showed me that someone else is always driving and He said to stop letting others drive me to unknown locations and get in the car He has provided and drive myself and listen to the one person who knows my destination and can give me the right directions, God Himself.

He showed me in a vision a beautiful white car and led me to the driver's side of the car. When I asked, shouldn't He be driving? He said no, because He gave me free will, which means He lets me drive while He gives me directions. It is up to me to follow His directions and He will navigate and tell me which way to go.

He told me to stop following other people, especially when I am not aware of where they are going. Stop following other people's dreams, other people's ministries, other people's ideas, and other people's habits and follow after God. He wants to lead me where He wants me to go, help me achieve the dreams He has for me, have the ministry He wants for me, and give me the right ideas and help me let go of old habits.

So many times, as Christians, we tend to look at other Christians to be examples of what we should do, how we should act, what we should say, our appearance, etc. But God is saying follow the Lord Jesus Christ and listen to the Holy Ghost for the plans and instructions that He has for us.

Chapter 9
THE DREAM II
March 20, 2007
9.5

While in prayer this morning, the Lord God gave me a new revelation about "the Dream." Several years ago, I had a dream about a fashion show I was supposed to be in. It had been a recurring dream. There were three parts to the dream:

- 1st part is I am always distracted, which makes me late.
- 2nd part is being late, which causes me to have to rush to get ready, but it never works out.
- 3rd part is disappointment that I missed the show.

Although the original interpretation of the dream was about the distractions in my spiritual walk with God, preventing me from participating in His plan and His work in the earth to save lives, today He gave me a new revelation about it. God is trying to take me to a new level in prayer. He wants to take me behind the veil but every day I miss my appointment — not due to lack of prayer, but because of not doing it correctly.

In the first part of the dream. I am distracted - Every morning after waking up, the first distraction I face is the temptation to sleep longer. The second is lots of thoughts running through my head about a variety of things from the day before, finances, work issues, etc. When I begin to pray, my mind wonders because of these distractions causing me to lose my train of thought on what to pray.

In the second part of the dream, I am rushing to get ready - This makes me late getting started in prayer, causing me to do a quick prayer and rushing to get to God to ask Him to prepare me for the day, then say thank you, and quote a few scriptures, then put in my petitions.

In the third part of the dream, I am disappointed - After getting up from prayer, there is a feeling of emptiness and disappointment as if nothing has been accomplished, as if missing my appointment with God. While in my prayer time I try to do (put on) things I think will work (me dressing myself). But again, I am choosing to walk in darkness (not having understanding) without wisdom (not having the knowledge of how to pray successfully). By surrendering to the Holy Ghost, He will prepare me for my appointment each day with an audience of one, the Lord God Almighty. Going upon the runway before an audience of one is like going behind the veil for an appointment with God.

HOUSE BEAUTIFUL

FROM TRASH TO TREASURE
Featuring
THE MASTER DESIGNER, GOD, OUR FATHER IN HEAVEN

My life has truly changed because of my walk with Jesus. He pursued me and helped me to rededicate my life to him many years ago despite me making a mess of my life.

There are times in our lives when we have to start over, make a change, get rid of old things and get new ones. Why is this? Because <u>we</u> are always changing. As we grow naturally, we have to make changes. We start school, change schools, graduate from school. We get jobs or start careers. We get married, start families. We have kids and these are just a few of the changes we go through in life.

Not all the things we go through are good. We tend to make a lot of wrong decisions, bad choices, we trust the wrong people and things happen to us. Because of this we have times in our life when we need to start over. We need to move forward in life. This requires that we make changes in our lives. The best change I made was to surrender my life to God.

As you can see from these pages, I have been on an amazing journey with Jesus. He has changed everything in my life. My decisions put me on a road to destructions. I thought I knew where my life was going, but through a series of bad choices, it led me to a dark place. If God had not come to rescue me, there is no telling where my life would be today.

God had a plan for my life that involved taking all the negative things and all the good things and put them together and make a beautiful tapestry of my life. He turned the trash that I had made of my life into His treasure.

It's like moving into a house that needs to be renovated. The structure is in disrepair and needs to be completely redone. The foundation is cracked. The walls are in need of repair. It needs a new roof and flooring. You move in and start making renovation. First, you need to assess the damage and determine what changes need to be made. Come up with a plan for the renovation and decide on a budget. Then you can remove all the old things that are currently in the house. Once that is done, then you can start making the necessary repairs that need to be made.

You need to start with the foundation. Determine if it can be repaired or if it needs to be replaced. Then go to the walls and repair any cracks or holes. There are some walls that need to be torn down. Then you can move on to the roof and replace it if necessary or make whatever repairs are needed. Then you can move on the things like painting the walls, fixing the floors, replacing cabinets and fixtures, sinks, tubs and toilets. Installing new appliances etc. After that comes the fun part. The decorating. Putting in the furniture, hanging curtains and art on the walls. Bringing in plants and lighting. Putting out all the decorative pieces. These are the things that turn a house into a home and change a dump into dream house.

The same is true in our spiritual life. There are a lot of changes that need to be made in our life once we give our lives to Christ. It took a while for me to get here because God had to rebuild my house. He (the Holy Ghost) moves in and starts making the assessment of what needs to be fixed, repaired or changed. The first thing is He gave me a new foundation (Christ). Then He tore down some walls (pride, anger, a false sense of who I am). He added some permanent fixtures (power and authority over our flesh and the enemy). He cleaned out some closets; there was a lot of junk in there (low self-esteem, disappointment, a broken heart, covetousness, envy, and much more) Then He decorated my walls with love, joy, peace, long-suffering, gentleness, goodness, meekness, faith, and temperance. (Galatians 5:22, 23) He gave me a new security system (the Holy Ghost). And He Himself is the roof that covers and protects it all.

God wants me to understand who He really is. He is a Master Builder who can take nothing and make it something. He can turn trash into treasure and take the broken pieces of our lives and make them whole again. He can make our House Beautiful and He is the potter, we are the clay.

Never underestimate what God can do in your life. He wants to help you accomplish the dreams He put in you and with God all things are possible. So now it's time to start your own amazing journey with Jesus and let him transform your life.

I would like to say
<u>Thank You</u>

I want to thank a few people who really came to my rescue in writing this book. They helped me get started, face challenges and overcome obstacles. They offered advice and encouragement.

<u>First</u>, I want to thank God our Father and the Lord Jesus Christ for helping me write the journals that turned into the book that I didn't even know was in me. He helped me to see that the journals could be a blessing to others as a book.

<u>Second</u>, I want to thank my nephew Adrian Patterson who put my journal notes together into book form. I could have never gotten it together without his help.

<u>Third</u>, I also want to thank our State Supervisor of women, Dr. Barbara Gillespie Washington. She truly encouraged me and let me know that this book would be beneficial to all who read it.

<u>Fourth</u>, I want to thank my new brother Ty Norris for giving me tips and suggestions to help get me to the finish line.

<u>Last</u>, I'd like to thank my publisher for her patience, advice and all her help in getting this book published.

www.ingramcontent.com/pod-product-compliance
Lightning Source LLC
Chambersburg PA
CBHW050144170426
43197CB00011B/1955